MW00977714

thinking of me.

1st run
unedited

Wisdom
While
Walking

TERRAN D. JACKSON

ISBN-10: 1482032198
ISBN 13: 9781482032192
Library of Congress Control Number: 2013902024
CreateSpace, North Charleston, SC

Memoirs of
Prayers and Dreams

Dedication

This book is dedicated to all the people who feel like they are in a hopeless situation and think that their present is going to dictate their future.

A special thanks to my brother, Byron B. Bryant Sr., who passed away before I completed this book. What an amazing title.
Jack, my lover and my best friend, thank you for being so patient with me all these years.
Quinton, Mom loves you until the end of time.
Mom, thank you for teaching me the power of prayer.
Peggy Magdon, thank you for speaking positive words into my life at an early age, and thank you for a lifetime of friendship.
To all the educators who taught me lessons that no textbook could have ever taught me, thank you.

Introduction

Life isn't all sunny days, and no one promised it would be. In this journey called life, I've learned not to fret the storm but instead to dance in the rain. I've learned to listen to the inner voice that speaks profound words. I've learned that in order to understand the lessons of life, I have to keep moving forward and holding on to my faith even when God doesn't answer my prayers in my time.

I've made it through the valleys. I've made it through aversive life situations. I've learned that when I walk in the steps that were ordered for my life, that is when I gain Wisdom While Walking.

Imagine Me

TERRAN D. JACKSON

Imagine me, a poor black girl who dreamed of

things I could not see

Imagine me, a doctor, a lawyer, and

still working on another degree

Imagine me, the one they said would never succeed,

who turned tragedy into triumph and now they believe

Imagine me, a broken heart, a wounded spirit too,

but I kept my faith knowing God would see me through

Imagine me, holding my head up high,

while inside my very being just wanted to die

Imagine me, not accepting my current situation as my destiny,

for I know there are things in life I have yet to do and see

Imagine me, being just like you; if I can make it,

I know you can too.

Now…

Imagine You!

Dreams and Prayers

*"**L**adies and gentlemen welcome to Johannesburg, South Africa. On behalf of our airline we hope you enjoy your stay." I can't believe I am here. Mama Africa, your daughter has come home after so many years. What a beautiful and magical place.*

"Terran, stop daydreaming. Where is your homework? You have missed several assignments. You have so much potential; you just have to put forth some effort."

"Yeah, yeah, I know, I can do anything or be anything if I just set my mind to it. Why you keep hassling me, Ms. Mag?"

"I hassle you because you have so much potential. I see things in you that you don't see in yourself."

I just look at Ms. Mag with a silent stare, but my mind is shouting at her. *"Do you see my struggles? Do you see my neighborhood in the projects? Do you have riots in your hood? Do you see the burning cars in the middle of the street? Do you see that I'm tired of watching my badass sisters and brother? You don't even know me!"*

I don't know why this white teacher acts like she really cares about me. She can't understand me, she don't know my struggles. I feel like I'm in prison in Marina Village. Nobody is leaving this place. Even the basketball players leave for college and end right back here in the Village. The Village has been my home for as long as I can remember. I write about the strife in my life. I pour out my emotions onto paper. This was my therapy long before I knew what therapy was.

The early years of my life seemed fun as a naïve little girl. I can remember very vividly my first day of kindergarten. Ms. Carolina seemed like the sweetest teacher I had ever met. She had those grandmother qualities. I can remember feeling like a big girl because I was old enough to go to school and my siblings were at home being babies: Byron Three and Wanda One. That's what we called them. It's funny how I can vividly remember many things, but there are times in my life that are totally blank, like a deep dark abyss that has held many years of my life. How can one remember kindergarten and not remember periods thereafter?

Even at an early age school seemed to be a sanctuary from the tumultuous life of the housing projects. School was the place that allowed me to be a kid without thinking about the troubles of the world. Kindergarten soon came to an end and it was time for graduation. I had successfully conquered this milestone. I felt so important and pretty all dressed up. My forehead was shining like somebody had slapped me with a fried chicken leg. I felt like I was the only child that was graduating and everyone in the audience was there to see me shine. I had memorized the pledge of allegiance and recited it very proudly. Ms. Carolina told me that she had never seen such a little girl with such a deep and loud voice. My mother sat so proudly—but where was Willie B? Was he even there to see his baby girl graduate? How I wish I could remember. I hope he was there. His first baby girl was shining like the bright stars on a clear summer night. This would be the prelude to his many absences. But I was still Daddy's little girl.

A family trip to Coney Island was filled with fun and lots of laughter. Anything that was wrong in my life at the time was overshadowed by the laughter and rides. I was on top of the world as I rode the merry-go-round, waving to my parents. Byron and Wanda were too young to ride the horsey like me. Daddy was taking my picture as I showed off my pearly whites. Whenever the camera came out, I was dead center waiting for a photo.

Slowly the laughter and smiles faded away. There was chaos and confusion. There was screaming and shouting. I found refuge in my closet and covered my ears. I wished the cussing and arguing would stop. Eventually it did, but then the silence seemed so loud. I waited a little longer before I emerged from the closet, making sure it was over. I knew it was over when I heard my mother crying and then the front door slammed. My father was gone. This was the first of many times

I wished I were in another place, a nice quiet place with peace and harmony.

School was the place where I found peace, laughter, and happiness. In first grade, I was such a star. Mrs. Albermonti had her students involved in many community activities. My name and picture were in the paper. I participated in the holiday parades down Park Avenue. I smiled and waved every step of the way, and people were calling my name. What an ego boost! But then the parade was over; the cheering had stopped. It was time to go back to the place I most dreaded: home.

My great escape came in the summer of 1973. I left Bridgeport, Connecticut, to spend a summer in Florida with my grandmother, who was affectionately known as Mama in our family. I don't know why my mother put me on an airplane all by myself. Once again, I was smiling from ear to ear. I was flying alone. I was told not to talk to anybody, and the airline stewardess would take good care of me and make sure that only my grandmother would get me on the other end. The crew was very attentive to me and I felt like a little princess. They gave me my first set of many wings.

I'm walking through a long tunnel holding the hand of a stranger. People are rushing to get out. The nice lady holding my hand is telling me we're almost there. My heart is racing because I know somewhere at the end of this long tunnel will be my grandmother. I can see the end, and there are a lot of people standing around, looking over people's shoulders. "I see her!" Quickly I let go the hand of the stranger and run toward my grandmother. The stranger runs after me, calling, "Wait!" I run into my grandmother's arms. The stranger tells my grandmother that she can't take me until she shows her some identification.

My grandmother snaps sarcastically, "Do you think she don't know her grandmamma?" She put me down and pulled out her billfold and showed the lady her driver's license. We make our way outside to the parking lot. I can hear the airplanes flying overhead, and as I look up, I wonder where each plane is going. But then a familiar face catches my eye.

"Uncle Bernard!"

"Hey, Terran, girl, you flew on that big ol' plane by yourself?"

"Yup, I'm a big girl."

We're driving down I-95 from the Palm Beach Airport to Delray Beach. We arrive at Mama's house. I open the old wooden screen door that squeaks as you push on it. I run in and go straight to Mama's bedroom and sit on the bed.

"I know you not to sitting on my bed!"

One thing you never do in Mama's house is to sit on a made-up bed. It was off limits.

Uncle Bern brings in my suitcases. I had a cute little pink vinyl set. Mama told me I could unpack later, and she showed me that she had a drawer for me to put my things in. "Come on; let's go let Ruby see you." We go outside and she yells across the fence, "Ruby...Ruby!"

My cousin Ruby-Lee comes out and says, "Paul, who that you got with you, is that Ten Cent?" My great uncle gave me the nickname Ten Cents because he said I wasn't bigger than a dime.

"It's me, cousin Rube! Where is Reggie?"

"Reggie...Reggie! Come on out here; yo cousin here."

I was so glad to see my cousin Reggie. We played together all summer long, and sometimes we went fishing with my grandmother. Reggie was being raised by his grandmother along with his brother Darryl. They watched out for me like I was a younger sister.

"It's time to go inside and eat. Ya'll can play tomorrow," said my grandmother. It was time for dinner, bath, and bed. Going to bed was what I dreaded most. I was still wetting the bed at night, and I didn't want my grandmother to know. The next morning I woke up in a panic because I indeed had wet the bed. I had to tell my grandmother, but I was so afraid. When I got up, I washed my face and brushed my teeth. I quickly washed up in the sink. I didn't want her to hear the water running in the tub. I could smell breakfast being cooked in the tiny kitchen, and I could hear my grandmother humming an unfamiliar song. She hummed these tunes all the time. I said good morning like everything was ok. She fixed my breakfast and set it on the table, and then she went into the bedroom to make the bed. I held my breath for what was coming next. "Terran, come in here, girl." I got up from the table and went to stand in the doorway of Mama's bedroom.

"You done wet my bed?" she asked, but we both knew the answer.

"Yes, ma'am," I replied.

"You too big fo this. You gone mess up my mattress." I slowly turned and went to finish my breakfast. The secret was out, but how was I going to make it through the summer without wetting the bed?

"You can't drank nothing late at night," Mama said as she passed through the kitchen with the wet bed sheets in a bundle. "I ain't gone be washin' bed linen every day, na. Go in the bathroom and wash yo tail." I took a bath and got dressed.

I felt better after I got dressed in clean clothes because I was going to work with my grandmother. She worked for this white lady cleaning her house and making things nice and neat. I used to think she was a nurse. My grandmother wore a white uniform and white shoes. That white uniform was so clean and ironed so neat. When we arrived at her job, my grandmother reminded me to mind my manners.

"Oh, Pauline, this is yo beautiful granddaughter? She is a pretty li'l thing." Then turning to me, she said, "Would you like some candy?" I loved to go to work with my grandmother. She worked so hard, but at the end of the day, this little white lady would always give me some money and tell me to put it in my pocket and "don't tell ya grandma" she'd say with a wink and a smile.

I couldn't go to work with her every day, so sometimes I would stay with my cousin Reggie and play all day until Mama came home. Then the fun began...fishing. I think I went fishing with my grandmother almost every day except on Sunday. I loved going on the fish creek with her and her fishing buddies, one of which had a grandson about the same age as me. Lamont was Ms. Gussy's grandson. We played more than we fished. There was Ms. Pearl; I think she was the oldest of the bunch. I felt like a li'l old lady hanging out with li'l old women, laughing and telling stories about their last fishing trip together. When we arrived back home it was dark. My grandmother loved the fish creek so much she could've lived on it. She would clean the fish, gut them, and scale them. Some was put in the freezer and the rest she made for dinner. There was nothing like eating fresh fish.

Then it was time to take a bath and get ready for bed. My grandmother never went to bed without saying her prayers. I would see her struggle to get down on her knees. I never heard her say anything but a slight whisper that I could never understand. I got on my knees and said my prayers out loud. I thought God wouldn't hear them if I whispered. "Now I lay me down to sleep, I pray the Lord my soul to keep, if I should die before I wake, I pray the lord my soul to take. God bless Mommy, God bless Daddy…Amen!" At the end of this prayer, I whispered and asked God to keep me from wetting the bed. I remember closing my eyes real tight and squeezing my hands together real tight.

It was daylight and the bed was dry! I felt so good! I ran into the kitchen to tell Mama good morning. She spoke before I could tell her my good news. "You in the kitchen and didn't wash yo face?"

"Yes, ma'am." I ran back to the bedroom, pulled the covers back and felt the bed just to make sure it wasn't wet. It was as dry as it could be. I washed my face, brushed my teeth, and sat at the table ready for breakfast.

"Hurry up and eat; we got to go pay bills today." I loved to go pay bills. My grandmother drove all over town to pay each and every bill in person except the insurance bill because the insurance man came to the house. I felt like a big girl. We had a system for paying bills. My job was to take the bill inside and hand it to the person behind the counter. Some counters were taller than I was, and when I got there, I would get on my tiptoes and slide the bill and the money across the counter, and the person on the other side would look over and see me, and smile. I would wait for the receipt and head back outside where my grandmother was waiting for me. We would take off to pay the next bill. At the end of the day, we would stop for some ice cream.

As we went from place to place, we made many stops alongside the road. I was a spotter….a spotter for aluminum cans. We stopped every few feet for the cans. I would jump out the car, grab them, and throw them into the back seat. Once we arrived home, my grandmother and I would go into the backyard, smash the cans, and put them in huge plastic bags. She said that smashing the cans made them weigh more and you could fit more in a bag. This routine went on for the entire summer. Then it was time to take the cans to be sold. I got a share of the profit.

The other highlight of being with my grandmother was I had many jobs. My other job was to lick the green stamps we got from the grocery store and put them in the little booklets. After we had a lot of booklets filled, we went to the green stamp store to shop for little things. Mama gave me so many books that I was able to buy something for myself.

My favorite moments with my grandmother were on Sundays. This, the holiest day of the week, was the only time she drank, and it was always Busch beer and Hennessy. Her brother, Uncle Floyd, would come from Palm Beach and they would sit around drinking and talking like they hadn't seen each other in years. This was my first taste of beer. My grandmother would always say, "Just a li'l swig." There they sat drinking and smoking cigarettes.

There was one thing I could never figure out about my grandmother. I don't ever remember her going to church, but she always sent me with my cousins. She drank on Sundays like clockwork, but she always prayed. She never went to bed without getting down on her knees and praying. What a contradiction.

One Sunday after Uncle Floyd left, she and I were sitting at the table. She was working on her crossword puzzle and I was drawing. She spoke the most prophetic words into my life—words I held dear to my heart and never shared with anyone until I was an adult. I was talking about growing up and being rich one day. She affectionately said, "You'll never be without; you're a child of the harvest." I had no idea what that meant at eight years of age, but I knew it meant something because she said it with such conviction.

Too soon, the summer came to an end, and it was time to return home to 427 Columbia Street, Bridgeport, Connecticut. I can vividly remember arriving in Florida and seeing my grandmother's face, but I can't remember returning home. I don't remember going to the airport, and I don't remember my mother's face when I arrived back home. There are many periods in my life that I can't put it all together. As I grew up, I came to understand that those were dark periods of my life. Not long after returning home, it was time to start school. My mother took us school shopping. She bought us what seemed like a lot of clothes. I was so ready to return to school. School was safe and it was a place of peace, away from the dysfunctional environment at home. Going to church also seemed to give me peace. It was there that I learned to pray my way through aversive life situations.

It was October, and for my birthday, my mother bought me my first ring. It was so special because it was my birthstone. In early November, I became sick. My limbs began to swell and my body ached all over. It was painful to walk. It got so bad that I couldn't walk up the stairs. I had to crawl, and my feet were so swollen I couldn't put on my shoes. I don't remember having a fever, but I remember being in so much pain. My mother took me to the hospital and they couldn't figure out what was wrong with me. My fingers had swollen so bad that they had to cut my new ring off. I felt like my world had just ended. They admitted me to the hospital, and I can remember being in what I thought was a cage. The bed had a wall of bars on all four sides. I cried because I was in pain, and then they wanted to take my blood. The needle seemed longer than a ruler. I was in the hospital for two weeks. Gradually I began feeling better, and there was no swelling or other complications. I can remember my mother being upset because they couldn't tell her what was wrong with me. I don't remember her staying any nights with me—maybe because she had to go back home and take care of my siblings. I had several episodes like this, as did my brother. We had to go to the doctor every week for them to draw blood and run tests. This became so routine that we looked forward to going to the doctor to get lollypops and stickers.

After several visits to the doctor's office and many tests, a breakthrough finally came. My brother and I were diagnosed with sickle cell anemia. My parents were told that my brother had the disease and I had the trait. My mother would pray day and night for complete healing for us. The pastor prayed for us. After the diagnosis, the doctor's visits were reduced. I remember my mother talking about the cold weather and stress being factors of this disease.

My brother and I learned to live with the disease, and despite the number of days we missed school, we both continued to excel. My classmates would always make cards for me with well wishes. If stress was a factor in triggering this disease, it seems like I should have spent more time in the hospital. My parents' arguments and fights seemed to increase.

Winter was my favorite time of the year. There was no keeping me inside. We would go sled riding and play in the snow until our fingers and toes were numb. I found out later that my father had stolen the sleds. The sleds and many other items we got for Christmas were all stolen. I guess he did what he thought was the right thing to do to ensure we had the things we wanted. Although we lived in the housing projects, I didn't know we were poor. I wore Stacy Adams shoes, and my parents sent my clothes to the dry cleaners because they said it would keep them in good shape longer. It was years later that I realized I was poor. How could I be poor? My father drove a new Camaro and then upgraded to a big Cadillac. Is poor a condition or a state of mind? Who could drive a brand new Caddy and live in the housing projects? Surely not a poor person.

I could not figure out why we couldn't move out the projects if we were not poor. Even though we had all these things, we still lived in Marina Village where there were riots in the streets and people getting killed for no reason. This was a place where broken-down cars would sit unnoticed for months.

I prayed for better days, but what were better days when this was all I knew? From an early age, I felt stuck. Nobody seemed to be leaving. I continued to pray.

Now I lay me down to sleep I pray the Lord my soul to keep, if I should die before I wake, I pray the lord my soul to take. Lord, please take me out of this place. Dear God, if you can hear me, please answer my prayers. I know I haven't been the best child, but please hear me. Hear my cries. They say ask and it shall be given, knock and the door shall open. Lord, I'm asking and knocking—please hear me. Star light star bright, first star I see tonight, I wish I may I wish I might have the wish I wish tonight. I wish to have my own big house. I wish my mother would leave my father. I wish for a better life. Amen.

It was the dawn of a new day, and with each day, I hoped that things would change. I patiently waited for God to answer my prayers or to give me some kind of sign. Each day came and went, and still there was no response from God—no answer to my prayers!

"Terran, get your lazy ass up and come go to the store." I hated the tone of my father's voice. It didn't matter what he said; that voice did something to my soul.

My father fought with my mother on a regular basis and degraded her every chance he got. I'd had enough! My brother I plotted to kill him. How bad could life be when we were planning to kill my father or even to do him bodily harm? We planned to use a rope and trip him down the steel stair. My brother was all for it at one point. Then he said, "What if he doesn't die from the fall? He's gonna kill us all in here." I thought long and hard about what he said. He was right. I thought of other ways to get this man out of our lives. But when I saw my mother taking him back each and every time, I knew she would hate me for killing her husband.

Days turned into years and I continued to excel in school. In grade 8, I set a goal to make perfect attendance. I wanted to do something my parents could be proud of me. On many occasions, I went to school sick, but I was determined to make my goal. I succeeded in accomplishing this goal.

During one summer, I started to volunteer at Park City Hospital. I proudly wore my red and white striped uniform. I can remember my brother telling me once that I really thought I was a "real nurse." I took my job seriously. I wasn't getting paid one red cent, but the fact that I was helping others who seemed to appreciate it gave me such gratification. I was awarded several certificates for the number of hours I had volunteered. Going to the hospital also took me away from the dysfunctional home I so dreaded being in. It was another escape, and I was helping people without dreading it. "Thank you" was sincerely spoken and greatly received.

I kept telling myself that there had to be a way out of the housing projects, but I didn't know anyone with a road map to show me the way.

High school was a very confusing and tumultuous time. I woke up to the role of motherhood, yet I had birthed no child. Expectations were demanding. I didn't want to be a mother to my siblings. I wanted my freedom! My mother and I became enemies and I didn't understand why. Nothing I did ever seemed right. Her solution was to send me to my father for a few days. I was now living with the man I despised so much. It wasn't an ideal situation, but I wasn't under my mother's roof anymore, and my anger turned from my father to her. It was during this time my father took me to the Kool Jazz Festival in New York. I felt special and grown up. To my disappointment, shortly afterwards he sent me back home. There I was back on Columbia Street. There was no escaping this place!

Star light, star bright, first star I see tonight, I wish I may I wish I might have the wish I wish tonight. Dear God, please hear my prayer and help me find a way out of this place. Dear God, they say ask and it shall be given, knock and the door shall open.

I prayed for better days. I prayed that Mother would get the strength to leave my father for good. I prayed for somebody to love me. *Please show me a way, dear God.*

After years of praying and going to church three or four days a week, I still didn't hear from God. My friend Michelle and her family were preparing to move out of the projects and into their home on Chopsy Hill Road. I became so angry because I just knew God had gotten it wrong or made a huge mistake. To add injury to insult, my friend invited me to her new house that sat on top of a very steep hill. I remember walking through the front door and thinking somebody had really made it out of the projects. As she took me on a tour through the kitchen, I recall seeing a dishwasher for the first time. It had a glass front door, and I asked her to start it so I could see how it worked. She told me she couldn't because it wasn't full, and they couldn't waste the water because that would make the water bill too high.

We never paid for water in the projects. We never paid any bill except rent and the phone bill. It was at this point that I felt second-class to my friend. First, she had passed the exam and made it into Tech High School, and I had only scored high enough to be a part-time student, and now this—she was living in this house. Our lives were worlds apart now. We didn't see each other very often after that, and I felt like an abandoned puppy. I returned home to the familiar place that seemed to be my destiny. I found the strength to continue praying. Day in and day out, I prayed. I started reading romance novels as an escape, hoping that one day Prince Charming would rescue me from this place and I would live happily ever after.

After my mother's failed attempts to reconcile with my father, she made a secret announcement. "We are going to move to Florida, and I don't want you to say a word to nobody, especially your father." We were so excited to start a new life but sad that we would have to leave our friends and all that was familiar. This was not an easy process, and there were many delays and setbacks. I knew it was too good to be true. Here we were, out of our apartment and living with the next-door neighbor, my mother and four kids confined to one bedroom. We had gone from bad to worse! The angrier I became, the more I began to pour out my feelings onto paper. I was writing long before I knew this was my therapy—my escape.

The moment finally arrived for us to leave, but not without incident. My boyfriend at the time really didn't want me to leave, and he decided to take an overdose of pills and ended up in the hospital. How could I leave him in this condition? What would happen to him if I did? What would happen to me?

These questions slowly faded as the realization grew that God had finally answered my prayers! We were really leaving Bridgeport, Connecticut, and Marina Village.

I eagerly anticipated arriving in Florida to start a new life. The train ride was long, but we made it! My grandmother was there with open arms. We stayed with her for a couple of months. She only had a small two-bedroom house which she and my uncle lived in. Now there was an additional five people living in this small house. There was nothing to call our own; nothing seemed familiar. Things began to get tense. My grandmother loved us, but it was hard with seven people living in this small place with only one bathroom. My mother and grandmother were at the end of their rope with each other. I didn't know why we didn't have a place of our own.

Then the call finally came. We were moving into Carver Estates. The name sounds very luxurious, but it was just another housing project. We moved in and got settled to the best of our ability. We didn't take any furniture from our old house and there was nothing to start with. I really can't remember where or how we acquired furniture, but bits and pieces started to come in. I thought I would like this new change, but it had its challenges too. School was no longer a place where I found peace and refuge. The only person I really knew was my cousin. Slowly it became a little better. I was now in my junior year, and this is when I met the love of my life. I couldn't wait to go to English class to see him. He was short and fine with bowlegs. His jeans fit his butt perfectly. I didn't think he even noticed me. In fact, I know he didn't. He didn't even ask me to go to the senior prom with him. Instead, he took another girl. How could he be interested in somebody so stuck up? I wished it had been me. Why didn't he ask me? The school year was coming to an end and still he said nothing except a quick "hey" when he came to class. I had such a crush on him, but I just couldn't let him know.

As fate would have it, our paths crossed again. This time he asked for my number. We talked for hours each day. I knew he was the ONE. Our relationship took a slight change. He had decided to enlist in the army. I was in my senior year of high school, but he promised to come back home and get me once I completed high school.

It was the end of the school year, and I had failed. I couldn't graduate. Many people wrote me off and said I wouldn't amount to anything. I thought otherwise. We felt like we couldn't be without each other, so I moved to Alabama with him. We got married at the courthouse. I was now Mrs. Denson with a military ID card and privileges. Shortly after I arrived, I enrolled myself in high school. I was determined to get a high school diploma. I couldn't leave my books in the car because my husband was embarrassed that his wife was still in high school. He even went so far as to lie and say the books belonged to a friend of mine. I never could figure out why he wouldn't be proud of the fact that I went back to school on my own, proud of the fact that I had enough in me to want more.

Living in Alabama was a big adjustment for me. It was the first place where I experienced racism. I had heard stories, but I had never experienced it until then. I was walking around in a store at the mall when I noticed this little white lady following me around. She wasn't offering to assist me so I asked her if there was a problem. She replied in the nastiest southern drawl I had ever heard, "We don't like your kind in our store." It felt like the devil himself was speaking to me. I stood there for a moment in shock as I watched her walk away.

Married life wasn't what I had dreamed it would be. I was trying to focus on finishing school, and living on one income was very challenging. I had painted a perfect picture of married life to family members and friends, but it wasn't so great. In reality, there was no food in the apartment. We weren't even making it from paycheck to paycheck. Things got so bad that my husband would go into the dining facility on base and steal food to bring it to me. He would do this for weeks until payday came around. I couldn't let anybody know how I was suffering mentally and physically. I did the only thing I knew how to do and that was to pray. I was eighteen years old living life as an adult, and failing.

Soon it was time to leave Alabama. My husband got unaccompanied orders to Germany. This meant that the army was not going to pay for me to move with him. After returning to Florida to drop me off with my family, we decided that we would pay for my ticket so we could be together.

I found Germany to be a beautiful but depressing place at the same time. The country was amazingly beautiful, but it was cold and gray all the time. My soul danced the first time I saw the sun. I stood in the window with my eyes closed and absorbed all the sun's rays. The summers were also mild and short—a vast difference from the long, hot Florida summer days.

Just as I started to make peace with this country and accept it, I was wishing and praying I could leave. The honeymoon was over and I had to deal with grown-up issues. The picture of a perfect marriage was suddenly changing before my eyes. My husband was seeing another woman. He came home with perfume on his clothes that didn't belong to me. To add insult to injury, he bought me the same perfume. I knew he was seeing another woman, but I could not prove it. I know I wasn't crazy. Since he wouldn't admit to the affair, I went into detective mode. I learned those lessons from my mother early in life. One day I told him I needed the car and I drove him to work. After dropping him off, I reset the odometer to see how many miles it was from work to home, home to work. I took every route possible each way and documented the miles. Then I drove to the next base in Stuttgart and back.

The next day he called from work and told me he was staying late for basketball practice. When he arrived home, I didn't smell the perfume, but my stomach still had knots in it. If he was still seeing her, he must be showering somewhere else before coming home. I waited until he fell into a deep sleep, and then I went out and searched the car. I wrote down the miles on the odometer and continued to search the car. Then a thought popped into my mind, and I looked in the spare tire compartment. There it was—a washcloth, towel, and soap. Yes, he was busted! I ran back into the house and interrupted his sleep and showed him his stash I'd found. Oh, I forgot I'm crazy, at least according to him as he hurried to explain that he had just put it there for showering after practice, and he wasn't hiding anything. I also told him that the woman he was seeing lived in Stuttgart. His eyes grew so big and round, he looked like a deer stuck in headlights. An argument ensued that lasted all night and went until morning. He would not admit to any wrongdoing. I broke every piece of crystal in the house that he had bought. I threw glasses and plates and busted the wall. He became physical and tried to pin me down. We both were tired. I couldn't shed another tear. He got ready for work and left me there with this mess to clean up. This would be the first of many physical, verbal, and emotional confrontations between us. I kept wishing I could leave, but where would I go? I couldn't go back home. That would be a sign of failure.

Every day I walked up the mountain to a little catholic prayer booth I had discovered there. I asked God to help me, and to give me peace and guidance. I asked Him to help me get out of this place. I went every day and the situation remained the same. The fights became more violent and more frequent. I finally called the military police and had him removed. It was at this point I just wanted to die. Thoughts of suicide raced through my mind. There were no pills to take, but I found a plastic razor in the bathroom. I turned the stereo on, and then I sat on the bathroom floor and asked God why He had not answered my prayers. Well, He must have heard me, because the razor was so dull it didn't break the skin on my wrist. It was at that point I heard God so clearly. He said, *"Hold on; trouble don't last always."* I questioned God and what I'd heard, but I kept hanging on, waiting for a better day.

The fights continued for a two-year period until I finally had enough. I went to my husband's commanding officers and told them I wanted them to give my husband a direct order to send me back home. Shortly after this meeting, my husband had to take a drug test, and it came back positive. He was informed that he would be discharged from the army. I felt sorry for him, but I also felt guilty that I had brought attention to him and caused his dishonorable discharge from the military.

In January 1986, I was on my way back to the United States not knowing what I was going to do. I was headed back to the place I dreaded most. I was back in the projects with my family and things were still the same. I felt like I was suffocating and couldn't breathe. My husband was home, broke, and ashamed. He wanted to reconcile and try working on our marriage. I agreed. I moved from my mother's apartment into his mother's house. It was crowded there, and we had no privacy. After a month, we moved in with his father. It was a little more private, but it still didn't settle with me. There wasn't a plan on getting our own place. I knew my husband was into drugs but I didn't realize how addicted he was.

One day, the little bit of money we had was missing. He blamed his father who was a good decent man with a good job. Why would he steal our money? Then the few things we had in storage started to disappear. There were lies after lies being told. I continued to pray and ask God to help me and deliver me from this place. I wept, wailed, and cried until I had no more tears.

A change had to come.

I started to feel stuck and hopeless once again. I only had a high school diploma and didn't know what to do with my life. I continued to hold on, and I reminded God that He had told me in Germany to hold on because a change was going to come. I continued to pray. It seemed like the more I prayed the worse things got. My husband and I argued and fought even more. I left my father-in-law's house and went back to the only place that was familiar, the place I dreaded the most, but where I knew I would be accepted. I was back in the projects.

One day out of the blue, I went to the army recruiter's office. I enlisted in the United States Army. When I asked how soon I could leave, they told me I was on the deferred entry list and couldn't report until June. June?! I wanted to leave right away before I lost the courage to leave. They told me the next start date wasn't until June. I said okay and signed my life away promising to report in June. This was March, and I had three months to wait. What was I going to do in the meantime? I reported to Miami for my physical. My heart was racing because I knew if I didn't pass the physical I could not be in the military. As I stood in a long line in the hall with only a cloth dressing gown, I looked down at my feet. My heart began to race. I remembered hearing stories about people not being able to join the military if they had flat feet. I didn't know if this was a myth or real, but it was enough to send me into a panic attack.

I prayed inwardly, *God, please let me pass this physical. Please don't let them notice my flat feet. Dear God, you said ask and it shall be given. I am asking you, Father, to show favor in this situation. Dear God, please hear the prayers of your child in the name of Jesus.*

Although I prayed, my faith was weak. I still had much doubt and was very nervous. Soon I was at the top of the line. I'll never forget the Asian doctor who intoned "NEXT" like it was a call to death. I got on the scale and he noted my weight on his chart. "Place the back of your heel against the wall," he ordered. He noted my height: five feet five inches. Then he looked down at my feet. I had scrunched my toes to make it look like I had an arch in my feet. He took the ruler he had just used to measure my height and then tapped the knuckles of my toes. I released my toes back to their normal flatness. "You have very flat feet," he stated. "You know you cannot join the military with flat feet like that." I felt the tears well up in my eyes. This was my only chance to get away, and I was going to be denied because of flat feet. "Please sir, I know I have flat feet, but I know I can be a good soldier, and I know I can make it in the military. I've never had problems with my feet. Please sir, my whole life is based on me getting in. Please sir, give me a chance." He paused for what seemed like an hour. He must have seen the despair in my eyes. "Okay, I'm going to clear you for duty."

"My God, thank you, Jesus" was all I could say under my breath.

Once I got outside, I thanked God profusely. For the first time in years, I felt like God was hearing my prayers—not just hearing them but answering them. Yes, yes, yes! I'm leaving this place! I went home to tell my mother. For some reason she did not believe me, even after I showed her my enlistment contract.

Soon it was June 15, 1986, and it was time to pack my bags. I was heading off to boot camp. My mother cried and my neighbors wished me well. I took a long train ride with other soon-to-be soldiers to report to training. My life would forever be changed. I arrived in Columbia, South Carolina and got off the train. It seemed like from that moment I would never walk again for the next eight weeks. Every time I moved, it involved running. I had my first encounter with a drill sergeant who got so close to my face I thought he wanted to kiss me. He yelled, "What kind of haircut is that?"

"A Mohawk," I answered.

"Faddish hairstyles are not allowed in THIS army!" he yelled. The next time I took a shower I washed out the gel and looked like a plucked chicken. Normally I would never be seen dead looking like this. But I looked around and all the other females looked just as bad or worse.

I was stripped of everything. I almost didn't recognize the person I saw in the mirror. I have come to learn that sometimes in order to move forward and get ahead, one must be stripped down to nothing in order to be built up into something new and fresh.

Basic training seemed like hell. It was hot and miserable. Then one day I looked at myself in the mirror, and realized that my body was being transformed. My mind and thoughts were being transformed. I was mentally and physically stronger than I could have ever imagined. I was walking with my head up and very confident. I felt like telling the drill instructors to bring it on! If I could survive the projects and an abusive marriage, surely I could deal with anything they threw at me. The days turned into weeks, and the weeks into months. I could see the light at the end of the tunnel. Finally it was here: graduation! I marched so proudly. Another accomplishment; another goal met.

I watched as other soldiers were greeted by family members and friends who had come to celebrate in their success and accomplishment. I had no one there to congratulate me or to tell me I'd done a great job. My heart felt a sense of sorrow, but I told myself I'd done a great job! I had passed phase one in the military, even though some back home didn't think I would make it that far.

There was no time for feeling sorry for myself, as phase two was about to start. I was bused to the other side of the base for Advanced Individual Training (AIT). I was going to attend classes to teach me the job I had enlisted for. There was some relief from the rigors of boot camp, but not much changed. We still had to endure early morning wake-up calls and PT, and now there were classes to attend. The job I enlisted for was an Administrative Specialist, 71L. The biggest part of my training was to pass a typing test along with learning administrative regulations, forms, documents, and procedures. If I couldn't type twenty-five words per minute at the end of the eight-week course, I would have to take it again. I practiced and practiced, but I wasn't making the mark.

As time went on, I was still making too many mistakes. I was determined to pass this exam. I began to do what I knew how to do best. *Dear God, I know you didn't bring me all this way to desert me. Dear God, please help me pass this exam. I know I'm not meant to go back home. Please help me, Lord.* The next day I went to class and it was time to take another practice test. This time our instructor told us to do a hand-eye coordination exercise before we started the typing test. We stood in place and marched, extending our arms high. We did this for five minutes and sat down to take the test. My words per minute had increased but I was still making too many errors. I practiced this exercise over and over and it seemed to be working. I prayed even more and harder every time.

Dear God I'm so close.

It was examination day and I woke up feeling confident and good. I felt like I was entering a ring for the heavyweight title. When I sat down to take the test, I declared inwardly, *I shall not be defeated. I am a child of God, and He did not bring me thus far to leave me.* My fingers were moving faster than they had ever done before. Even when I thought I had made a mistake, I just kept going.

"Time up and stop," said the instructor. There was silence in the class. Some faces smiled with relief while others looked sad and disappointed. After class, some of my classmates asked, "How do you think you did on the exam?"

I said, "I'm done."

The next day the result list was on the wall. My eyes scanned down the list for my name, and there it was: PVT Denson—Go. Yes, I was graduating! I fell to my knees, and cried and thanked God for showing me favor. I wanted to do a little shout in the hallway and get my praise on.

The following week was relaxed and easy. We spent our time cleaning the barracks and getting ready to ship out. The next day we got our first permanent assignment. My stomach had butterflies wondering where I was going. South Korea was my assignment. I knew nothing about Korea, but I had already lived overseas for two years, so the thought of going to another country didn't bother me. I wondered what my mother would think of me being away yet again.

Graduation day came, and once again, I didn't have family there to cheer me on and congratulate me for a job well done. For the first time I was ready to go home. Not because I was homesick, but to show everybody I had done it—I was moving on. I wanted to show my father that he was wrong when he told me I wouldn't be shit and wouldn't amount to anything. Those words were the driving force that kept me going.

I arrived back to Florida proudly wearing my uniform with my first pin on my chest. I was greeted by neighbors and family members like I was a celebrity. I prepared for church service and donned my uniform again. The pastor acknowledged me during the service. I knew I had succeeded as the community praised me for a job well done. After being home for a couple of weeks, I was ready to get started in my new life and face whatever it had in store for me. Being home for a month seemed like a lifetime. I spent most of my time with my nieces and nephews. Most of my classmates seemed to have fallen off the earth; they were either dead, strung out on drugs, or in jail. I couldn't relate to anybody at home anymore. Our paths were so different now.

A Change is Gonna Come

I arrived in Seoul, Korea in November 1986, and it was cold. I felt so lost in this new world; so uncertain of what was in store for me. As all the incoming soldiers sat through our briefing waiting for our final assignment destination, I went outside to smoke. After a moment, a Staff Sergeant Jackson approached me and asked for a cigarette because they didn't have this particular brand in Korea. As he held out his hand, I just stood there and looked at him as if to say, *Are you crazy?* I vividly remember the lame line he used from a famous movie in response to my blank stare: "Do you want my hand to fall off?" I broke down in laughter and gave him one. As we talked, he informed me that he was responsible for sending incoming soldiers to their final assignment destination. He also added that if I was ever in the area to look him up and he would show me around Seoul.

Soon it was time to board the bus that was taking us to the train station. While waiting, this same individual showed up and asked if I was okay. He gave me his number and asked me to call him when I came back to Seoul. I found his flirting very flattering. He was an older man, and I didn't see a ring on his finger. I was thinking he just want a trophy girlfriend to kick it with. I took his number and thought I'd never see him again.

I arrived at Camp Humphreys and was shown to my dorm. I couldn't believe I was going to spend the next year in a tin hut that looked like a big storage area from the outside. I got in and met my roommate. She was an E-4 sharing the room with a PVT. We quickly set our boundaries and we were cool with each other. I got settled in, and it was time to do the job I had been trained to do. There were only three females in my company and a lot of young tall guys. I knew PT was going to kill me the first time. Although I ran on the beach when I was at home, I did it at my pace. Now I was faced with keeping up with these tall guys with long legs. I knocked out the first run like a trooper! The other females dropped off, but I pushed myself to keep up. It seemed like every bone in my body was in pain. I just wanted to take a hot bath and relax my muscles. That wasn't going to happen because we only had shower stalls.

My roommate wanted to take me out and show me the nightlife and the clubs. I declined the first couple of times. I wasn't the party type of person, and I felt guilty about having fun while my husband was back home and miserable, most likely. Although we were separated, I still felt guilty.

I finally gave in and went out with my roommate. What a blast we had. There were so many men to choose from. I danced until my feet hurt. I got so drunk that I don't remember how I got back to my room. I felt free and liberated! Going out once turned into going out every weekend. I partied like the world was coming to an end, and I became a regular in the clubs. I even started to hang out on Sundays, but I could still get up early Monday morning and do PT without missing a beat. One night one of the owners of the club, a woman named Sookie, pulled me aside, and asked if I was interested in making some extra money on the side. I quickly told her I wasn't into drugs or anything like that. She said no, it was nothing like that. She said that a Korean man who was a regular at the club wanted to get to know me and take me out. If I liked him, he would pay me to go out with him. I told her I wasn't a prostitute. She said it wasn't about having sex with anybody; I would just be his date. I agreed and met him in the club. He was a very well-dressed Korean man. We sat and talked business. He wanted somebody to accompany him to a few social events. At first, I was very leery, but being young, I agreed.

The following weekend would be our first meeting. I asked my roommate to go with me to the gate where he would pick me up. I wanted to make sure somebody saw me leaving with this man I will call Mr. Cho. We arrived at a social event, and I stood out like a pink elephant in the room. I was the only black person there. What could I have possibly been thinking to agree to this? The people were friendly and it was a very upscale event. I mingled easily being the social butterfly that I am. I couldn't understand half of what anybody was saying. The drinks were free and the music was nice for a Korean event. I danced with women and men alike and started to have a good time. Mr. Cho and I were apart more than together. When it was time to leave, he drove me back home. When we got to the base gate, he paid me as promised. He asked if we could get together again. I told him I had to think about it. I told him if he wanted to get in contact with me, he could reach me through Sookie at the club.

My roommate was waiting up for me to make sure I made it back safely. I told her about the evening and how he wanted to take me out again but I didn't think I would go out with him again. It wasn't me.

A few weeks went by and Sookie informed me that Mr. Cho wanted to meet with me again. I caved in and agreed. The money was too good to pass up. Each week I would go to my tailor and get new clothes made, and then I would have a pair of shoes made for each outfit. I continued with this arrangement for several months. I kept telling myself that it was okay because I wasn't having sex with this man. We had an agreement and we both kept to our agreement, but Mr. Cho wanted to see me more and more frequently. Instead of attending social events, he wanted to spend time alone with me. I couldn't take that chance. I declined and cut off our agreement.

One day while cleaning out my junk drawer, I came across Staff Sergeant Jackson's phone number that I'd written on a scrap of paper after meeting him when I first arrived in Korea. I went back and forth trying to decide whether to call him. I finally mustered up the courage to call him. I was sure he wouldn't remember me. It had been several months since we had met, and hundreds of soldiers processed through at any given time. I called him and reintroduced myself. I reminded him that he told me to give him a call if I were ever to return to Seoul. We set a date for the following weekend and I took the bus to Seoul. I called him when I arrived, and he claimed he had something to do and was apologetic for not being able to meet me at the bus station. All I could think was, *Yeah, right!* Well, I figured that since I had come all the way up there, I would make the best of it. I ran into a guy I had met when I first arrived in Seoul, and we went out for drinks and hung out together. I ended up staying the night with him and headed back home the next morning.

I called Staff Sergeant Jackson to give him a piece of my mind. He apologized over and over again and said he really didn't think I was coming. He asked if he could make it up to me, but this time he would make the trip. I thought, *Okay, if he is willing to come see me, why not?* We set a date. I wasn't sure about this and got cold feet. This time I stood him up.

At this point, we decided to talk over the phone for a while. Jack's voice was heavy and sexy. He seemed very intelligent and had a great sense of humor. Our conversations made me more curious about him. I wondered why he seemed interested in me. He is twelve years my senior and a single parent raising three kids. I didn't think we would have a lot in common. We finally agreed to meet again. He asked me to come back to Seoul so that he could show me around, and he explained that this would be easier because of the situation with his kids. He also agreed to send me the bus ticket this time. How could I not try again?

I arrived at the bus station, and this time he was there to greet me. I couldn't believe we were finally on a date. He drove around to various places and landmarks around Seoul.

Our last stop was the Seoul Tower. We got on an exterior glass elevator that took us to the top floor, which overlooks the city. The elevator was crowded, and I turned my back to take in the view. Jack put his hand around my waist at the small of my back. Inside I smiled at his gesture. As we exited the elevator, he took me by the hand and led me out. When we exited the building, he started taking pictures of me. I felt like a kid and enjoyed the moment. We ended the day with dinner. He must have been a regular there because the people greeted him as a friend, and he spoke Korean fluently. I was so impressed but thought he was just showing off. It was time to head back to the bus terminal, so I thanked him for a wonderful day. He then gave me a passionate kiss. I really didn't expect it, but it felt so right.

We continued to see each other. I loved the way he made me feel. He made me laugh and made me feel beautiful as he snapped pictures everywhere we went. I loved taking walks with him and holding hands.

After several dates, we decided to take it to the next level. We checked into a hotel, and Jack gave me a beautiful burgundy lingerie set. I was very shy at first, but he made me feel comfortable. The experience was unforgettable. He touched my inner soul as no other man had done before him. We became regular customers at this hotel. He explained that he didn't want his kids to meet me until he felt we were serious about our relationship. I had so much respect for him and the way he considered his children in everything he did. After spending the day together, he would go home to make sure his children ate dinner and were off to bed before he returned to the room and to me.

After several months of this routine, Jack took me to his house for dinner. I met his three children and his mother-in-law who was there assisting him with the kids. It was a nice dinner. He told me that his middle son had just been suspended from riding the bus for trying to jump out the window, and now he had to take him back and forth to school. His oldest son was a mild-mannered kid who talked a lot. His daughter helped me clear the table and load the dishes in the dishwasher. This was the first of many occasions we were together like a family. Every time I departed, I was sad. This particular time when he drove me to the bus station, he kissed me as he always did, but then he said those famous words that made my stomach feel like there were butterflies inside. He said, "I'm falling in love with you." I didn't know how to respond. Instinctively, I wanted to say I felt the same way. I told him that I cared a lot for him, but I couldn't tell him the same thing. I apologized and he assured me that it was okay. I kissed him and got on the bus.

Those words consumed my mind the entire ride home. My feelings were mixed. I smiled as I replayed the words in my thoughts over and over again. Then a feeling of fear consumed me. I was still legally married, and here was another man telling me he was falling in love with me. I was on a rollercoaster ride of emotions, and I didn't seem to have control over them. I decided to sit back and enjoy the ride.

Jack and I continued to see each other and things seemed to be getting more and more serious. My heart ached when I wasn't with him. I felt safe and secure in his arms. He seemed to make my world perfect and pure. It felt so right—too right. I started to wonder if this relationship was a way to pass the time for both of us. I wondered if I was allowing this older man to seduce me; or was it real? The more we were together the more he told me he loved me. I finally reciprocated his response. As soon as I said the words "I love you," I couldn't believe what I had just told this man. He hugged me tight as if he had been waiting for those words to come out of my mouth. I had said them now and couldn't take them back.

In my heart, I wanted to love and feel love. I had built a wall around me after my experience with my husband. He too was charming and had told me he loved me even though we fought like enemies. What did love really feel like?

I suppose Jack must have loved me because he was supposed to leave in June, but he sent his family back and extended his stay in Korea for six months so that he could be with me. I really didn't expect him to do that nor did I ask him to. Now I was really scared of where this was going. After months of dating, he came to see me. We had a good time, but I knew it would be for the last time. At dinner, I told him I couldn't see him anymore. I will never forget the look on his face. My heart sunk. He asked why, what was going on, was I seeing some-one else? I told him I just needed to breathe a little bit and I needed some space. I needed to find me. It seemed like we were moving so fast. I walked him to his car and we kissed passionately, and then I said goodbye. He said don't say good-bye but see you later. I went back to my room and cried until my eyes were swollen. I wasn't sure if I had done the right thing. I had prayed for a knight in shining armor, a king, and now I had just run him off. But we didn't belong to each other. We were still married to other people.

I moved on with my life. I went back to partying and having a good time. I started to see another guy who was my senior in age and rank. He had two young kids back in the States. It seemed like all these guys had kids or were married. It was a way to pass the time I had left on my tour.

I finally decided that I was going to file for a divorce from my husband. We'd been separated for almost a year and I didn't plan to go back to a place where God had delivered me from. I called him to tell him that I wanted a divorce, and he pleaded with me not to do it. I cried on the phone when I heard the pain in his voice. But I knew this was something I had to do. We hung up and I felt guilty—guilty for living my life and having a good time while he was still unemployed and living at home with his mother. The guilty feeling quickly subsided as I thought of the hell he put me through for two years. I deserved to be happy and enjoy my life.

Things were going well until I got that dreaded phone call from the American Red Cross. The only time they contact people is when there is an emergency back in the States. The Red Cross told me my mother needed to reach me, as there was a family emergency. I quickly ran across the street to my office and called my mother. Tearfully she said she needed me to come home because my father was in the hospital from a gunshot wound in his back and they didn't think he was going to make it. I began to scream and cry. She told me that the shooter was my brother and the police were now looking for him. I regained my composure and told her everything would be okay and I would be home as soon as possible. As soon as I hung up the phone, I called the only person I knew I could talk to. I'm glad we remained friends even after I had broken his heart. He told me how to go about taking emergency leave. I then informed my First Sergeant of what had transpired at home. He confirmed the Red Cross message, and then he set everything in motion for my return emergency leave. I arrived in Seoul to take the long sixteen-hour flight back to Florida. My constant friend was there to greet me. He hugged me tightly and kissed me like never before. I was reminded why I had such deep feelings for him.

As I sat on the plane, I wondered what my father could have done to set my brother off in such a way. They had a volatile past and were more like friends than father and son. They got high together and even shared some of the same women. My father's idea of teaching my brother how to be a man was to teach him how to manipulate women into giving him whatever he wanted. He introduced him to a life of crime, drugs, and women. This was my father's legacy to his son.

I landed after the flight that seemed like it would never end. When I arrived home, I was welcomed by my family members. When I inquired about the details surrounding the incident, nobody could give me the answers I needed. There were many speculations, but they were just that—speculations. My brother was still on the run from the police. He'd had his share of run-ins with the police from a young age. I laid down to rest to muster up the strength to go see my father the next day. I was so worried about the man who gave me life, but also who told me I was a slut and wouldn't amount to anything in life.

We arrived at the hospital in Miami. He was in the intensive care unit, and I was told that he would not be able to speak because he had a tube down his throat. My heart was heavy as I thought how critical he was. I took a deep breath and entered his room. I became angry and numb all at once. At his bedside was one of his many women friends he had left my mother for. Anger consumed every part of my body. I was angry at this woman for being in the spot that my mother should have been in, angry at my father because he hadn't changed at all, and angry at my mother for having me fly such a long way and for not letting go of this man who had not an ounce of respect for her. After I regained my composure, I asked the girlfriend to leave so that I could have a moment with my father. My mother stayed in the room. I looked into my father's eyes and I began to cry. I could see the pain in his eyes. Tears started to flow from his eyes. He was so shocked to see me. He couldn't believe that I had made such a long journey to come see him. He motioned for paper and pen because he could not speak. With the little strength he had, he wrote the words *I love you*. They were simply words without a meaning to me. Nobody who loves could cause so much pain and chaos in other people lives.

I was home for fourteen days, and I never went back to see him. I told my mother she was obligated to visit him because he was her husband, but she should not expect me to go back. I guess what infuriated me the most was that my father had given this particular girlfriend's daughter away at her wedding. I was his first daughter. I could never understand how he could give away somebody else's daughter before having the honor of giving away his first-born girl. I think most every girl dreams of her wedding day and marrying her prince, and being given away by her father. I wondered if I was too much of a dreamer. Why was life always so cruel? I was glad when it was time to leave to return to Korea. I was ready to leave the drama I had forgotten while being away. I was ready to get back and get on with my life—back to Korea, the land of the morning calm.

I called Jack to let him know I was back. I didn't go into much detail about my trip, but it was good to hear his voice again. He always seemed to make things better, and could always make me smile. Once again, he assured me he would always be there for me.

After a few weeks had passed, I stopped seeing the other man I was dating, as it was getting closer to the time when my tour of duty in Korea would be finished, and soon I would be leaving the country. I couldn't go without talking to Jack, the man that I spent so much of my time with. I wanted to see him one last time before I left, but he thought it would be too painful for him. I gave him my mother's address and number, and told him that if he should ever want to reach me, he could contact her. He told me he had been accepted into Drill Sergeant School, and he was excited about it. He would be stationed in South Carolina, and I was headed to Maryland. Once again, we said, "See you later—not goodbye."

I was headed back to the States while he remained in Korea for another month. I arrived home just in time for Thanksgiving. As much as I dreaded going home, there was always some gratification in returning to show the family I was still alive and well, and making a life for myself. There had never been a visit home without some form of drama, and this time was no different. I met my husband, whom I hadn't seen in over a year. I told him I would be moving forward with the divorce once I was settled in Maryland. He told me he wasn't going to sign the papers because he didn't want a divorce. Of course he didn't. He had nothing going for himself. I was making a life for myself, and I had shown him and everyone else that I was very independent. I felt like he would be dead weight pulling me down and suffocating my career goals. He was content with being at home and living with his mother. I on the other hand wanted to see the world and all it had to offer.

I prayed and asked God for guidance on my decision. I didn't get an answer, but I continued to pray. *Lord, you know my heart. I just want to be happy and to be with a man who appreciates and loves me for me.*

I arrived in Maryland in December 1987. It was cold and snow covered the ground. I got settled into the barracks, but it wasn't long before I requested to move off post into my own apartment. I could do this because I was married, though nobody knew that my husband and I were separated. I didn't have a car to commute back and forth to work so I rode in with a friend. I just couldn't stand the thought of life in the barracks after living in them for a year in Korea.

I needed my own space.

One day I got a call from my mother telling me she had gotten a letter from my friend in Korea. My face lit up with the thought of him actually contacting her and inquiring about me. Shortly thereafter, I received a letter from him. I couldn't believe he actually found me and wrote me.

7 Jan 88

HAPPY NEW YEAR! :-)

Hello Baby-Love,

Yeah I'm still after you. I hope this letter finds you in the best of health, both mentally & physically. I'd give anything to be from you right now. I never thought I'd think of you the way I have. I hear you soft sweet voice saying, "Hi" over & over my mind. No one has ever impressed me like you did Babe. What the fuck did you do? :-)
I miss you so. I tried to call your mothers house but the number is changed and the new number is disconnected. I'm doing O.K. and I start school tomorrow. I like S.C. so far, but I still think of you. Do you ever think of me? When I left Korea I did'nt want to see you because I was afraid of my feelings for you. You were the only female I could'nt walk away from. I never did get your letter. Babe, I may never have you again but I want to always know that you're O.K. and all is well. You know I have no shame. When people ask how old I like Korea, I say it was O.K. except a lil 22yrs old Rocked my world. :-) Write me soonest Babe. I spent alot of time with the kids while I was on leave. It felt good. I did'nt go home for Xmas. That's when I tried to contact you. I bought a '85 MAXIMA. Yeah!, I said never a V.W. :-) Have you lost anymore weight? Tarran I want to hold you and lick your face so bad. :-) I've met a few people here I knew in Korea. It snowed here today — 4 inchs. I'm ready for school, I want to get it on. I plan on taking leave when I finish — near 15th. Possibly if you're not all tied up with someone like a pretzel we can hookup.

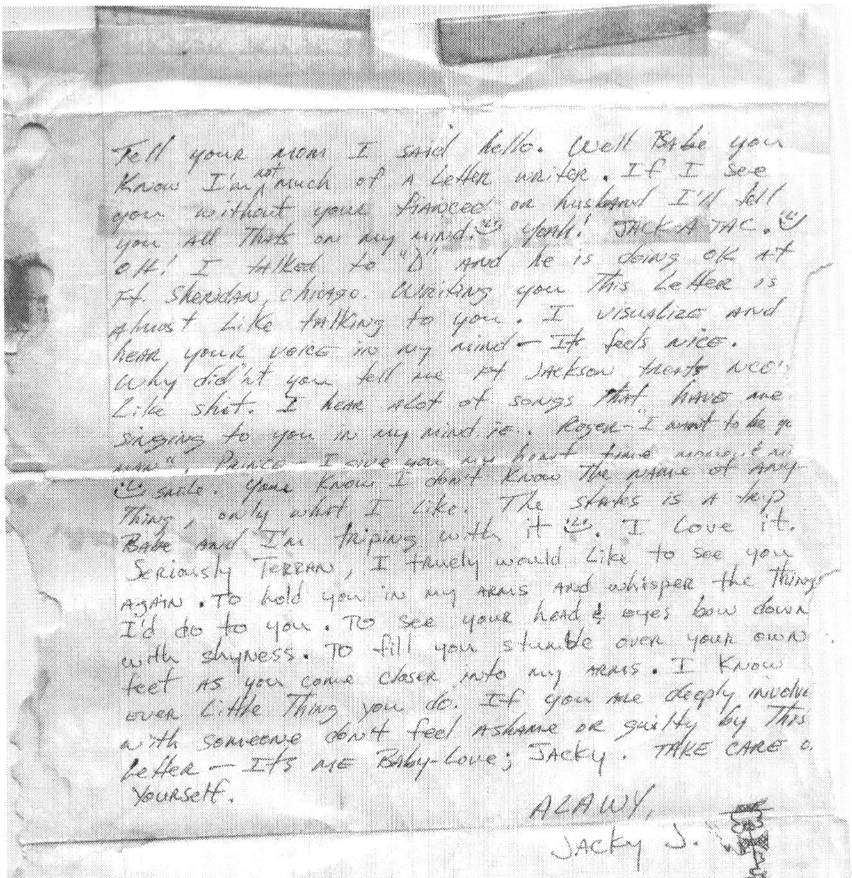

The tears flowed down my face as I read his sweet letter, and I smiled as I thought of all the good times we had—all the times he made me laugh and feel secure. It was like we never missed a beat with each other. How could a person know me so well and love me the way he did in such a short period of time?

I felt an urgency to contact him. I knew he was in training, so when I called I said I was Major Denson. I figured no one would question an officer. My heart raced as I just told the biggest lie. The person on the other end told me to hold on, and then I heard his voice—his deep sexy voice that I had become so familiar with. I was so excited I thought I had peed in my pants. His tone was a little short with me and I was confused at first, but then I realized that he couldn't talk openly. I gave him my number, and later that evening the man I knew surfaced. We talked for hours playing catch up. I didn't care about the long distance cost. I just wanted to enjoy this moment. We continued to communicate while he was in training and he made plans for me to come to see him when he completed his course.

As promised, he sent me a ticket to fly down to South Carolina. This trip brought back so many memories, as this was where I started my military career. When I stepped off the plane, I saw him there waiting for me. I ran into his arms and gave him the longest passionate kiss. I couldn't believe we were together again. As usual, I cried tears of joy! This felt so right. We departed the airport and got a hotel room. He was currently residing in the barracks, and that's not the place to have a reunion.

The passion was still as strong as ever. We stayed up late into the night talking about our lives, and we shared what we both wanted in the future. I told him I thought of him every day, and told him I was foolish for running him out of my life. He echoed similar sentiments. We agreed to start seeing each other and to try having a successful long-distance relationship. We agreed to take turns with the commute and break away as often as time would allow us. We committed to each other with the exchanging of rings, which we put on necklaces we each had. The weekend ended too quickly and it was time for me to depart. This time there wasn't sadness but a yearning for the next visit.

He made the trip to Maryland to come see me. While visiting I told him that I needed assistance with obtaining a car. I asked if he would co-sign for me. He said yes without hesitation. We went to the dealership and I picked out a little red Pontiac LeMans. Jack's name was the only one on the loan. Since we were not married, he asked me to sign a promissory note stating I would make the payments so that I wouldn't ruin his credit. I agreed, as I thought it was fair and the right thing to do. Now I didn't have to depend on anybody for a ride to work.

We continued to commute back and forth to see each other. I had a friend who had family in South Carolina, and we took turns driving down to help each other pay for gas.

Jack came to visit me again, and while parked in a quiet area, he gave me my ring back. He said he thought I wasn't ready for a committed relationship and one that involved his three children. He said he loved me too much to make me feel like I would be burdened with a pre-made family. I again started to cry and asked why he was saying this after all we had been through. I told him that if I wasn't sure about us, I wouldn't have pursued him and maintained the long-distance relationship. He kissed my tears and apologized for making me cry, and he kept the ring.

When I went to visit him in April, I told him I had some decisions to make in the coming months. I had to reenlist in June or request to be discharged. I told him we would both receive orders sooner or later, and we could be assigned to totally different regions of the world. I asked him what his intentions were regarding our relationship. In one breath, I asked him to marry me so that we could remain together; otherwise, I was going to reenlist, and we would deal with the different assignments when the time came.

To my surprise, he said, "I would love to marry you."

We were both still married to other people at the time. I told him that if he was serious, he should get his divorce first. My rationale behind such a statement was if I got divorced and he changed his mind, I would lose my pay benefits of having a dependent husband, whereas even if he got divorced, he would retain his benefits because he had dependent children. He agreed whether he thought it was fair or not.

In June 1989, I made a huge move by leaving the military and moving to South Carolina. I completely stepped out on faith. I gave up on my career to be with the man I wanted to spend the rest my life with. I had no guarantee that it would work. We had never even lived together. I had no guarantee he would even marry me.

When his divorce was final, I began to work on mine. It was the best $500.00 I ever spent. In four months, I returned to Florida for the final divorce hearing. The judge asked me if I wanted to resort to using my maiden name I told him no, I was getting married again soon and it would change anyway. He had a very puzzled look on his face. I walked out feeling free! Now I could move on with my life.

Shortly after returning to South Carolina, I missed my period. I was excited but fearful at the same time. We knew we were going to have difficulties in getting pregnant. I'd had several surgeries and had gone through infertility treatments. I had prayed so many years and asked God to let me conceive. I became sick to the stomach and my mother shared her infamous dream of fish. She told me I was pregnant. Our family believed that if a person dreamed of fish, someone close to that person was pregnant. I finally went to the doctor and confirmed that I was indeed pregnant. I was so excited that after all these years I was going to be a mother.

My joy turned to sorrow shortly after finding out I was pregnant. I hadn't even made it to my first doctor's appointment. I was driving home from work and felt this awful pain in my lower back. I thought I was tired from the commute. I made it home and went to the bathroom and there were spots of blood. I immediately called my mother. I was scared and crying. She tried to console me and told me a little spotting is normal. As the evening went on, the bleeding became heavier. I called my mother again and she advised that I go to the hospital. Jack came home immediately, and I was told that I was having a miscarriage, and soon they would be taking me to the operating room to give me a D & C. I cried out to God and asked why this was happening. Why, after so many years of trying to get pregnant, was this happening now when I was so happy with Jack? As I lay awake on the operating table, the doctor told me that she couldn't see a fetus. She said I was being prepped for anesthesia because I must be pregnant in one of my tubes.

I woke up in my room with Jack and a friend at my side. I didn't want to see her because she was a few months pregnant, and at that point, I resented her. Jack tried to console me the best he could. I had never cried for so long in my life. The doctor came in to tell me that not only had I lost the baby, but one of my tubes had to be removed as well. She tried to console me by saying that adoption could be an option for us. I didn't want to hear anything she was saying. I was young and healthy and knew I would give birth to my own baby one day.

I was home for four weeks recuperating. I cried myself to sleep every day. I felt like I was going to lose my mind. I told Jack that I needed help to deal with this. I prayed and prayed, and asked God why He had allowed this to happen. One day during a quiet moment, His answer came to me loud and clear: *"You prayed to be able to conceive, and I granted that prayer."* I didn't want to hear what I'd heard, but it was so loud and clear.

I changed the way I prayed. I prayed a more specific prayer. I asked God to allow me to birth my own child, and to please allow me to get pregnant again—please!

After dealing with this loss, Jack and I had to deal with the medical bills. I didn't have insurance since I was no longer in the military. We talked about getting married even more now because I didn't have insurance.

I started to plan a very simple wedding. We both agreed to get married in a church since neither of us was married in a church in our previous marriages. I was content with it being just the two of us and the preacher—or in our case, the chaplain. We were poor and we knew we couldn't afford a wedding. I bought my invitations from a party store and typed them on the typewriter. I couldn't afford a wedding dress so I bought a cream three-quarter-length gown from a prom store. I was happy with the simplicity of everything. Then

I thought about having a bridesmaid at my side. I asked my friend to stand with me. She already had a dress very similar to mine. Jack had his longtime friend as his best man. They didn't require a tuxedo because they both wore their army dress blue uniforms. We were set, or so I thought.

My wonderful husband-to-be wanted this to be as much like a complete wedding as possible. He wanted my oldest niece and my friend's daughter as our flower girls. Then he added my friend's son as the ring bearer. Everybody had clothing that was appropriate and we didn't have to spend money on those items. I ordered a very small two-tier cake with the bride and groom on top. We were so broke that we couldn't afford a caterer. My mother made all the food and we had the reception in a small meeting room at one of the local hotels. There was only one thing missing on this very special day. I walked down the aisle alone. I would not give my father the satisfaction since he already had given away another woman's daughter. I thought of my brother, but he was incarcerated at the time. I walked down the aisle with my head up high the same way I had been born…alone.

As broke as we were, it was the best day of my life. We didn't have a honeymoon. We just stayed the night in a local hotel while our family members stayed in our apartment. It was official. I was now Mrs. Jack Jackson! Nothing else seemed to matter at that moment.

A few months had passed and I still found myself crying whenever I saw a pregnant woman. There was such a void in my life. Jack thought I was going crazy. I was frequently angry with him because he couldn't understand my pain. How could he? He had three beautiful children. Collectively we thought a change was needed for us. He requested an assignment back to Korea—back to the place where we met and fell in love. I needed this change. I wanted to get away from everything that was familiar.

We were off to Korea once again, but this time as a couple. Everything seemed nice and new. We were in an area neither of us had been assigned to before. It was in the southernmost part of Korea, which is near the ocean. I loved being close to the water. The water always seemed to soothe my soul and my spirit. We brought over Jack's middle son, who was giving his mother a hard time, and my youngest sister, who was the same age as Jack's son. They both stayed for a year before they returned to the States.

We learned of a wonderful fertility hospital in Korea. We made several trips to Seoul to see the specialist and took our Korean friend with us to help us through the process. I had a minor procedure done and was released from the hospital. We were going through the in-vitro process in an effort to conceive. After several attempts, I still didn't get pregnant. I was emotionally drained. We had been trying for four years and still nothing. I gave up on praying. I told God I didn't even have the energy to pray anymore. I had lost all hope. People kept telling me it would happen when I stopped trying to get pregnant. The strain of it all was starting to take a toll on our marriage. I had become obsessed with getting pregnant. I started to pray again and asked God for wisdom and discernment. All I could pray was, *Help me understand, dear Lord.*

Once again, I could hear Him plain and clear: *"I am in control; trust and lean on me."* Even though I heard His voice so clearly, I couldn't see tomorrow. My thoughts raged, *It is my body, and I am not in control of my own body!* God would answer, *"Hold on, my child, for I have not forgotten you. I hear your prayers."* How could God hear my prayers? The Bible tells us to ask and it shall be given. I had asked for so many years.

I took my frustrations out on Jack. I had no one else to blame. We seemed to argue more and more over the simplest things. One night I became so angry with him that I went to his job, found where the car was parked, and slashed three of the tires. I would have slashed all four but the military police were making their rounds and I didn't want to get caught. Everybody on this small base kept asking what happened to our car. I openly admitted to doing it. Jack's response was his crazy-ass wife did it. Over time, we looked back at the incident and laughed. We never seemed to stay angry for very long.

As we entered our last year of a four-year tour, I got a devastating call from my mother. My only brother was sentenced to death for armed robbery and for murdering a grocery store clerk. My world seemed to shatter again. He was only twenty-four years old. My mother was about to die from the news. I couldn't be there to comfort her. What could I say to comfort her? When I got off the phone,

I began to pray. I asked God to have mercy on my brother's soul. I asked Him to keep him safe. I asked Him for comforting words to share with my mother. A wave of emotions swept through me. I felt guilty for leaving home so early, and for leaving him behind to fend for himself. I was his big sister; he had always bragged about me. I was angry with my father who introduced him to this life of crime. It was his fault!

I couldn't stomach the thought of my brother dying in Florida's electric chair. *Dear God give me the strength to deal with pain. Please comfort my brother right now in the name of Jesus!*

In April 1994, we returned to the United States. Florida was our first stop. I was so glad to get off the plane, smell the salt air, and see the palm trees I hadn't seen in four years. Coming home was always such a love-hate experience, and this time was no different.

After getting settled, I went to visit my brother in the county jail. He was his usual upbeat self. He assured me he was okay and asked me not to worry. How could I not worry about the only brother I have? We spoke through the thick glass. I could not hug and embrace him like I wanted to. I put my hand on the glass as we spoke on the phone. Although our lives were worlds apart and a thick piece of glass separated us, I still felt so close to him. I told him to remember to pray. He laughed and said, "Sis I'm good; don't worry about me."

In a selfish moment, I told God I was sorry for what my brother had done, and though he was accused of taking the life of a husband and father, I asked God to spare his life. I departed the jail with a full and heavy heart. It was time to switch gears and focus on our new assignment to Atlanta, Georgia.

Neither Jack nor I had lived in Atlanta, but we were blessed in getting this assignment. It placed us in equal distance to his home in Washington, DC and my home in Florida. We knew this was where Jack was going to retire, and this would be the place to own our first home. We moved into an apartment while we started our search for a home. We decided to have a new house built just for us. We were excited with the idea of building our first home. This process was new to both of us. Finally, after five months of construction, we moved into our home. It was perfect in every way. Soon my emotions started to get the best of me once again. The house didn't seem complete without children—my children.

After five years of marriage, I finally conceded to the idea of adopting. We enrolled in an adoption class that lasted for ten weeks. I initially thought we would adopt a young child. However, after the ten-week session, I decided I would not feel complete if I missed out on the early parts of motherhood. I didn't want to just be a mom. I wanted to experience every part of motherhood as much as possible. We switched gears and changed our preference to adopting an infant.

We attended another six weeks of adoption class with another agency. We were grouped with three other couples who were in the same situation. We could relate to one another on many levels. For the first time I didn't feel alone. I had somebody who could relate to all that I had been through. We became friends and had get-togethers to get to know each other better. The first couple received their son. The second and third couple received their children soon thereafter. We wanted a little girl and the other couples had boys. Our social worker told us she had another boy waiting to be adopted. We declined and stated we would wait for a girl. After seeing how happy the other families were, however, we opened our options to a boy or a girl. When we informed our social worker, she said the same little boy was still waiting to be adopted. We made an appointment to meet him and his foster mother at the adoption center. When I saw his face, the tears flowed down my face. Many years I had dreamed of my baby, but I thought it was a girl. He had so much hair that he could pass for a little girl. He was so beautiful, and had the longest eyelashes I had ever seen. I fed him and changed his diaper. We spent several hours with him and decided he was the one. He was an eight-week-old very sweet baby boy. We informed our social worker that we wanted to adopt him.

We left excited and filled with joy. We went out and bought a car seat, and began decorating his room. We had little time to get ready, but we did it. The following week, we signed the paperwork and picked up our son. We named him Quinton Alexander Jackson. We informed our family of the addition to the family. My mother was so excited for me. I was the oldest child yet my younger siblings had already had children. I took a month off from work to bond with my new son. My mother and aunt came and stayed for a month after I returned to work. Our lives had changed for the better, and now everything was complete.

Quinton was such a perfect baby. He didn't wake up during the night nor was he a fussy baby. I felt so blessed to be his mother. One evening after I put him to bed, I fell asleep and awoke to a very bright light descending from the ceiling of my bedroom. It was my maternal grandmother, who had passed many years ago. My heart began to race when I saw this vision. Her face glowed as she spoke to me. She said, "I came to see the baby." I couldn't move. My body was paralyzed. I tried to scream but no words came out of my mouth. She left my room and I wanted to run to his nursery to check on him, but I couldn't move and became exhausted from struggling to get out of the bed. She returned to my room and told me he was a beautiful baby and everything would be okay. She then ascended to the ceiling just as she had come. It was not until she disappeared that I was able to move. I ran into his room and picked him up. He was breathing peacefully and seemed fine.

I had heard stories of people having similar experiences, but I had always doubted them. Now I was a believer in angels. It was such a profound experience, and one that I will always remember. I was at peace with the adoption process, and this experience told me it was right.

Shortly after Quinton's arrival, we had another addition to our family. Jack's twelve-year-old daughter came to live with us. She was very helpful with the baby and accepted her new baby brother. We were a happy family. This was short-lived and things began to change. She became very jealous of the baby she had seemed to love and became very disrespectful to me. I couldn't figure out why her behavior had changed. It became so bad that I didn't leave Quinton alone with her. I would tell Jack of the problems I was encountering during the day. He dismissed it and seemed to think I was exaggerating. As time went on, the behavior became worse. This sweet little girl I had known began to take on a Dr. Jekyll/Mr. Hyde personality. She was rude and unruly when we were alone, but when Jack came home, her entire personality changed to this sweet pleasant little girl again.

One evening I told Jack that we had just had a confrontation before he came home. He looked at me as if I was crazy and lying about his daughter. The situation put a strain on our marriage. I felt stuck in a bad dream that I could not wake up from. This went on for a year, and Jack could not, would not see what I was saying. I finally took a stand and told him she had to return to her mother. I further told him I didn't trust her around my son, and she had become too much for me to deal with. Reluctantly, he sent her back to her mother. All was normal again and there was peace in our home once more.

Shortly after that, we received a call from Jack's ex-wife stating that she was having problems with his middle son and she wanted him to come live with us, as she could not control him anymore. Of course, Jack did the proper thing and had his son sent to us. These were trying times for us. His son had problems with authority and with me. He was very rebellious and had a lot of anger. He didn't have problems with Quinton but with me. We had many altercations on a daily basis. All I could do was pray that God watched over me and my baby as Jack worked the night shifts. It became so bad that I had Quinton sleeping in my room and I locked myself in my room at night with a knife under my pillow.

I was afraid of his son's temper. He would come in and out of the house as he pleased. One day I arrived home to find this beat-up car in the driveway. I went into the house, and there were these thuggish-looking guys in my house. I had never seen them before. I went around the house to make sure things weren't stolen or missing.

Dear God, please deliver me from this situation. I can't stand the thought of living in fear in my own house.

It seemed like God was preoccupied with other things and did not hear my prayers. I came home to the smell of marijuana and hit the roof. I didn't want to confront him until Jack came home. I was so fearful that I told a friend that if anything happened to me, to have the police look for Jack's son. Many nights I went to bed thinking it would be my last night on this earth. I told Jack about all the incidents, and it seemed like everything I said was falling on deaf ears. I didn't want to give Jack an ultimatum because he was my husband, but I was getting desperate. I knew how he loved his children. But why should I be the one fearing for my life and living in hell on earth?

Dear God, please hear my prayers. You have never left me alone. Please give me guidance on how to handle this situation. I need your help, dear Lord. I asked you to send me my prince charming, my knight in shining armor. I thought life would be great. Why am I going through these trials, Lord? Dear God, please help me.

Once again, I heard Him: *"Stand!"*

Stand? Lord, please let me know better days are coming. Please give me a sign. You know sometimes I can be slow and miss your signs. Please make it plain for me to see and understand. Please give me a spirit of discernment. Lord please give me strength to deal with this child.

I could not—I would not let him know I was so fearful of him. I kept telling myself I had done nothing wrong; I am a child of God, and I know He is watching over me. Every time I made this declaration, I seemed to grow stronger.

As time went on, things got better. We learned how to tolerate each other. I became more comfortable letting him watch Quinton when I had to run to the store. Deep inside, I still wanted him out of my house. It was graduation time for him and I knew he had some tough decisions to make regarding what he was going to do with his life. He decided to join the military. He enlisted in the US Army as his father had done. *When does he leave; when does he leave?* The question played in the back of my mind constantly.

Six months after graduation, he was gone. *Thank you, Lord, for delivering me from that ordeal!* My house was quiet and in order again. We spent the next five years in peace and alone in our home. Then we received a call from my sister-in-law asking us to take in my nephew and let him live with us. He was heading down the wrong path, and she wanted us to intervene. How could I say no? I had promised my brother that while he was in jail I would help with his kids even from afar. Now we had a twelve-year-old living with us. It seemed as though we had a revolving door at our home, and there was a sign on the outside that read, *Come on in—the Jacksons can help with your problems.*

I soon came to realize that we had a purpose in each of the individual lives that came into our home. I prayed and asked God to give me a break, but God had His own plan. This process went on for several years with different family members sending their child/ren to live with us.

An Educated Woman

My life has always seemed to have its peaks and valleys. I try to plan my life as best I can, and it always seems that God has His own plan for my life. I have learned not to fight and struggle, and to accept things for what they are. But this lesson didn't come easily.

I made a five-year plan to resign from my government job, return to school full time, and take my son to and from school each day. What a tall order to juggle...

Dear God, you know my heart and my dreams. Please give me the strength to be a good wife, mother, and student. Give me the courage to succeed and overcome each challenge I encounter.

I resigned from my job and took a nine-month break before returning to school. I took my son to school and picked him up like the good stay-at-home mom I had always wanted to be. I became the class mom and served on all types of planning committees. This kept me busy until classes started in the fall the following year. Returning to a college campus at thirty years of age caused never-ending anxiety. I kept telling myself, *I can do this; I have to do this*. Each year brought new challenges. Trying to juggle a full class schedule and be there for my son and husband took a lot of energy and good time management skills. Many times, I felt like quitting and returning to work. However, I was not a quitter and Lord knows there were many who thought I couldn't do it and were waiting for me to fail.

I was so focused and driven while studying. I soon felt like I had lost my identity. I was no longer Terran but Quinton's mom and Jack's wife. I wanted to break out of this mold. My self-esteem was very low. Going to classes and being a room mom didn't require me to dress in a professional manner. I didn't have time for a social life anymore. All my time was spent studying, going on field trips, cooking, and cleaning. I wanted a break from it all.

Midway through working on my degree, I decided to take a cruise with a fellow classmate. We drove from Atlanta to Jacksonville for a three-day cruise to the Bahamas. It was a long overdue break. We had a wonderful time. We had a male cabin steward who was very handsome and had a Caribbean accent. I noticed he was extra nice whenever I requested something. He told me he was from St. Lucia and had been working for the cruise line for a few years. My classmate and I put our luggage outside the cabin and stood in a long line on the stairs waiting to check out, when I realized I had left my declaration paperwork in the cabin. I went back upstairs to retrieve the papers. As I departed the cabin, I ran into the steward and he signaled for me to come in the room. As soon as I was inside the cabin, he closed the door and proceeded to do a strip dance. Oh my, what an awesome body he had. He came closer to me and began to touch my body. I was so caught up in the moment. *This must have been how Stella felt when she got her groove back*, I thought. My other thought was, *I can't do this*. No other man had touched my body since the first time I was with Jack. After the brief sexual encounter, I quickly got myself together, washed up, and left to join my classmate. I didn't say a word and slept almost the entire trip back home. I was so overwhelmed with guilt. When Jack came home, he asked about the cruise. I told him it was good. He asked if I had behaved myself. I said of course. Deep down inside I was dying because I wasn't much of a liar.

I confided in a girlfriend about my encounter with the cabin steward. I told her I was feeling so guilty that it was killing me. I told her that I had to tell Jack. She asked if I was crazy. But I knew she didn't know or understand our relationship. Jack and I had made a promise to each other that if either of us ever had an affair, we would ensure protection was used and we would tell each other about it. Jack asked me several times if there was something I wanted to tell him. The last time he asked, I confessed of my wrongdoing. This could have ended our marriage, but somehow we made it through. It didn't happen overnight, but we made it. The trust was lost, but I knew where I wanted to be and who I was in love with. I prayed and asked God to forgive me. I asked Jack to forgive me.

I continued to pour myself into my studies. I needed another type of distraction. I started to seriously work on my artwork. This gave me a break in between studying. I cleared out an area in our basement and started to create pieces. I would work on a few pieces and return to studying. This system seemed to work out well. I wasn't putting all my time into books, and the art was a good distraction.

When people came to our home and saw some of the pieces on the wall, they asked why I didn't do this full time, and some even suggested I have an art show. I couldn't imagine having an art show or going through the process of getting my artwork out there for others to see. But everyone said the same thing when they saw my artwork: they said it was unique. Thus, I picked up the name Unique Art. I didn't license it or anything. I just signed each piece Unique Art by Terran. This was turning out to be a wonderful inexpensive hobby. I would go to the home warehouse stores to get broken/used materials. I wanted the pieces to be raw and natural materials. The other product that was free was brown grocery bags. All I had to buy were the paint and clay for pieces that displayed masks I made as part of the design.

One day I was passing a church that was having a bizarre, and I saw a sign that said they were selling booths for ten dollars. I told Jack that it would be a good place to show off my art. I set up my booth with a few pictures I had made. Many people came by and commented on how beautiful and unique the pieces were. Finally, a gentleman came by and looked at my art. He asked what made my art unique other than it being a different type of artwork from what one usually sees. I told him that I could produce the same piece of work several times, and none of them would be identical to the others because I don't measure colors or brushstrokes, or arrange the backgrounds the same. He said he liked my art and wanted to buy a piece for a friend who had just opened a business. I told him I promised he would never see another like it. He seemed particularly interested in one piece and asked what I was willing to sell it for. I was so surprised I didn't even really think about prices. I told him, "Since you are my first customer I will sell it for forty-five dollars." He agreed without hesitation. He asked if he could have it framed and enclosed in glass. I told him that framing would be expensive because the frame would have to be custom made since the pieces are not standard measurements. I also told him I didn't recommend enclosing the artwork in a glass case because the materials needed to breathe. He took my advice and thanked me. I was so excited. I wanted to sell something, but more importantly, I wanted to see what other people thought of this different kind of art. I called Jack and told him that I had just sold my first piece of art. He was equally excited for me.

When I returned home, I told him that was the only piece I sold, but I got a lot of positive feedback from people who didn't know me. I told him about the buyer, and then I explained how he had asked about having the artwork framed. Jack told me I should make my own frames since my art varies in shape and size. I told him I couldn't do frames; I didn't know how. He told me that he would buy me a miter saw as an investment for my art. I didn't even know how to use a saw or know how to cut the corners, but I figured I could learn. I took Jack up on his offer. He kept asking me about holding an art show. I told him I couldn't focus on that and school at the same time. He never asked me about it again.

I continued to focus on my college courses and working on my art in my basement. I went and bought framing wood and tried using the saw. Gosh, I made so many mistakes! I couldn't figure out the angles, and I couldn't figure out how to make it work around my pieces of art.

Then one day I had an idea that would make the pieces truly unique. I made the frames a part of the art. I attached the frames to the pieces. One could not remove or change the frames. I continued to work on the pieces and showed Jack each creation when it was finished. He asked me how I had chosen the names of the pieces. I told him the names didn't come to me until I was finished and I looked at the piece as a whole. I never start with a concept or picture in mind. I just create and then the name or title follows.

I hadn't shown many people my new framed pieces, but many were still asking about a show. I was in the middle of writing a research paper when it hit me. I ran outside and yelled down to Jack in the backyard. "It's time!"

"Time for what?" he asked.

"Time for my art show—I have it all figured out!"

When he came into the house, I told him my thoughts. I told him I would have the art show at the house. I would hang the pieces all over and allow people to flow from room to room to see the different pieces. I also wanted to give away some pieces as my appreciation for attending the show. I would have a drawing for a piece and I would have a game. I would have all the pieces covered up in black cloth and give everybody a list of the pieces, and they would have to find the piece throughout the house. The winner would win a piece of art. Jack was in favor of the entire concept except having that many holes in the wall from hanging the pictures. I told him they had removable hangers that didn't require putting holes in the wall.

It was time to do this, and I put every minute of my down time into this project. I worked on pieces late into the night. The titles came out of nowhere. I made the invitations and got them in the mail. The date was set and all was a go. I was excited about sharing my craft with others. It really wasn't about making this a career or making a lot of money. It was showing the world another side of me.

Dear God, you know my heart and my desires. I pray that this showing is in order with what you would have me to do. I pray that it is a success, not monetarily but in the sense of showing you in a nontraditional form. For all I do is to give you the glory. Amen.

It was time for the show. It was very intimate and personal without a lot of fuss. People met and mingled. Everybody was given a number that would later be drawn to win the piece I had titled "The Garden." Everybody was given a list of all the artwork on display. It was wonderful to hear the discussions around the pieces as people clustered around various works of art. Some titles were very obvious, but others were very thought provoking. They had people looking up and down, turning their heads from side to side. I smiled as I continued to walk around. I gave a history of the concept behind Unique Art and how it was birthed. "I know some of you have seen some of my work and insisted I have an art show; for some of you, that was years ago. It wasn't the right time back then, and I don't like doing something until I'm moved by God to do it. If I do something because man says it's time, then it will not have the same impact and the purpose will be missed. Now is the right time because it is God's time. Thank you for encouraging me!"

"FREEDOM"

This piece represents freedom from all things that bind us!

Freedom was the first piece of artwork I sold at my art show. I made everything by hand except the mat. The mask and chains are made of clay. The mask is also hand painted.

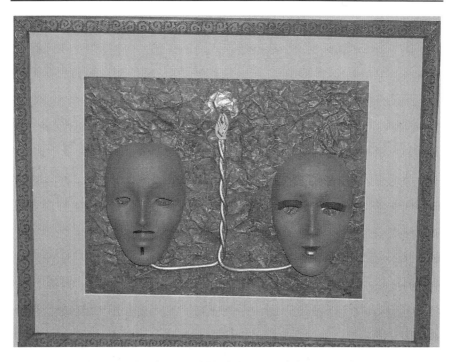

"ETERNALLY COMMITTED"

"AFRICAN SEASHORE"

"PARADISE."

The show was such a success. I actually sold more pieces than I expected to sell. I also had orders for custom pieces because I only had one of each on display. The most popular two were "Freedom" and "Who are you?" The latter is a black mask with a big question mark in the middle of the forehead. I wanted to create pieces that were thought provoking.

When I calculated what I had spent to make the pieces and what I had earned at the art show, I found that I had a surplus. I couldn't believe how successful it was. After the show, I returned to pouring myself into my studies again. Many people asked when the next show was planned. I smiled and said, "The next show is when God moves me to do it. If it never happens again, then I'm fine with that too."

Preparing for the show and studying really took a lot out of me. I was becoming so burnt out trying to juggle everything. In my third year, I needed to take a break. I decided to take the summer off and have elective surgery I had been contemplating for some time. I had been having problems with my back and going to the doctor on a regular basis for cortisone shots in my back for muscle spasms. My breasts were large and heavy. Carrying heavy books and art supplies around seemed to make it worse. I met with the plastic surgeon who agreed I was an ideal candidate for the surgery. He said that I would benefit from a breast reduction and would have much less back and shoulder pain as a result.

All the paperwork and pictures were sent to my insurance company, but they denied the procedure. I called the insurance company to inquire as to why they had denied it. Surely, the pictures themselves should have spoken volumes in approving the surgery, and my doctor's notes proved that I had a medical need due to my back pain. I said to the woman on the phone, "Ma'am, how could I not be qualified? My boobs are sitting on my lap; are you looking at the correct file?" After communicating with the insurance company and the surgeon, it was discovered there was a coding error on the paperwork submitted to the insurance company. I was then cleared to have the surgery. I had Jack film the before and the after of the surgery for documentation of the entire process. I was ready. The doctor came in to go over the procedure with me, and then he used a marker on my breasts to delineate how he was going to proceed.

I woke up in the recovery room in a little pain. I only had two questions for the attending nurse: was my blood pressure stable, and were my eyebrows still drawn on. I looked down at my breasts, which were bandaged tightly. I couldn't see them, but I could see that they were much smaller. After I had been in the recovery room for a few hours, my doctor came in to say everything had gone well during surgery and I should recover fine. He discharged me to go home and ordered me to return to his office in three days to have the bandages and drainage tubes removed.

I was feeling fine at home until the pain started to kick in. When it was time to go to bed, I couldn't sleep very well, even with the pain pills and the sleeping medication I had been prescribed. I could only sleep on my back, and it was very uncomfortable. Jack stayed home with me the first two days, but then he had to return to work. My dear girlfriend came from Augusta to assist in the healing process. She took me to my first doctor appointment. I was excited to finally see my new breasts. She held my hands as they removed the drainage tubes. Looking at my breasts and feeling the slight tug from having the tubes removed caused me to get lightheaded. They laid me down and I rested a moment. As I lay on my back, I looked at my breasts and was stunned to see how perky they were, standing straight up in the air. They looked so small in comparison to the breasts I'd had just three days ago. I was given an all-clear sign from the doctor. My friend and I went bra shopping. I couldn't believe I could now shop for the cheap bras with two-closures in the back instead of having to buy the expensive bras with four to five closures in the back.

My girlfriend returned home after spending a week with me. I had to change my dressing now. When I went to put on new dressing, I noticed the skin around my areola was peeling. I phoned the doctor and he said I should return to his office. He told me that enough blood wasn't getting to the tissue of the skin around my areola. He told me he had to cut away the skin because it was dying, and this had to be done to prevent an infection and keep me from completely losing my nipples. I was horrified. The problem kept getting worse. It looked like I was going to lose both my nipples. Each time I went to the doctor, he had to cut away more dying flesh from my breasts. During my last visit, so much dead tissue had to be cut out that I was left with deep, open holes in both breasts. The doctor kept assuring me that it would heal, but I would be left with a lot of scar tissue.

I said to him, "How is it possible for this to heal? I have a wide, deep hole in each of my breasts. How will those holes just close up?"

The doctor told me I had to change the dressings twice a day to keep the wounds clean and infection free.

"Doc, I can't do this. I hate the sight of blood, let alone an open flesh wound."

He told me I must change it twice a day in order to keep from losing my nipples and my breasts entirely. Thank God, Jack had the stomach to do this. I knew at some point I had to gather the strength to do this on my own. I did it while Jack was at home, and I got so sick, lightheaded, and nauseated. I thought I was going to pass out. I didn't want to look at my breasts, let alone pack all this dressing into the holes in my breasts. I did this ritual for over a month.

I was hoping my breasts would be healed by the time the fall semester started, but they weren't. Fall classes resumed and I had to take bandages with me every day just in case the drainage started to soak through the dressings. I managed to make it through the day without changing the dressings.

It came time for me to do my practicum and subsequently write my thesis. I knew I wanted to work with at-risk youth. My college mentor introduced me to the director of a non-profit organization that assisted youth in the community. This organization worked with the juvenile justice system in assisting troubled kids to obtain their GED, but it also provided supervised community service, assisted in helping students obtain work skills, and served as a reporting center for kids who were on probation. This organization has some of the roughest kids that society says will never make it in life.

I started during the summer program that taught the students a trade, and at the end of the program, we took over one hundred students from Atlanta, Georgia to New York and to Washington, DC. The program was a success. I spoke to the director and asked her about the possibility of employment once I completed my degree. She thought it was a good idea and told me to contact her at that time. When I completed my practicum, I wrote my thesis on juvenile recidivism and the core of this ongoing problem in our society. It was then that I felt it was my calling to work with and focus on the youth in our community. I wanted to make a difference in the lives of the youth that society considers beyond help.

I completed my degree in psychology and human services and graduated with honors. What an accomplishment! During the course of my studies, I learned so much about myself, particularly why and how I became the person I am. It was when I allowed myself to be open and honest and to face my demons that I had a profound cathartic realization that I am still a work in progress. I am not and never will be perfect by any means. But my goal in life was to become a better person and not allow my past to dictate my current or future situation. I learned to define my definition of success. For me, success is not defined by the letters that follow my name or the amount of money in my bank account. Instead, it is the conscious decisions, choices, and changes I make that help me be a better person while helping others do the same.

After an extended period of self-analyzing, I went back to the non-profit organization I had volunteered with to seek employment. To my surprise, I was offered a job as the Educational Coordinator with the GED/Life Skills program. This was totally different from the summer program I had worked in previously. I had an array of students to work with, including gang members, teen moms, and abused teens, and for some students this was their last stop before being sent to a juvenile correctional facility.

On my first day, I came to work in a suit and heels. The facility was an old garage in a strip mall area. When I was brought into the classroom and introduced to the students by the director, my first thought was *Oh my God, what have I gotten myself into?* It felt like their stares were burning a hole right through my body. I wasn't given a lesson plan or any real guidance. I was simply told that my job was to get as many students to obtain their GED as possible, and then in the life skills phase of the program, to help them transition into the employment.

I spent the first day observing the instructor and the students. These students were from all walks of life. Most were living in group homes for one reason or another; some were being raised by a grandparent; some were living with their parents, but because they were already in the juvenile justice system, they were mandated to attend this program; some were homeless; some found refuge in the program—and then there were the gang members.

After watching how the students interacted with the teacher, it was time for me to get to work. I introduced myself and told the students I wanted to meet with each of them individually. I had to know who and what I was dealing with. I had to know their stories. As I was speaking, half of them were talking and playing around. I dropped a book onto the concrete floor; the room fell silent. "It is rude and disrespectful to talk while I am talking. I will not disrespect you, and in return, I expect you to do the same. Understood?" My heart raced so fast, it felt like it was going to burst out of my chest. I knew I couldn't let them see the fear I had inside.

At the end of my first day, I concluded that in order to reach these kids, I had to make them respect me; then I had to work on gaining their trust. They had been told many things by many people. Most of these kids had low self-esteem because they believed the negative message that society had told them about who they were. They didn't expect to succeed because society had told them in many ways that they would never succeed. When I looked at these students, I was reminded that they were no different from me. I could have easily been one of them.

After my first few weeks of observing the program, I concluded that there had to be a better way to motivate these kids. As it was, they were teaching themselves the five area of the GED program: Reading, Writing, Math, Science, and Social Studies. To complicate matters, their ages and academic levels varied. I went to my director and asked for permission to try some non-traditional methods of teaching since these were non-traditional students. I asked to be allowed a range of technics to help the students to learn. I was pretty much given free range in how to help them obtain their diploma.

My goal was to use the required material and books along with real life events and non-textbook materials. For their writing portion, I used the required material as a starting point, but then I had each student write a brief autobiography and read it aloud to the class. To minimize their fear, I promised that I wouldn't ask them to do anything I wouldn't do. To put actions to my words, I wrote a brief autobiography of my life and read it aloud. At the end of my story, they thought I was lying about my past. They wanted to know how somebody from the "hood" could drive a nice car and come to work "on point" (wearing nice clothes) every day. I told them I didn't let my past surroundings dictate my future. As I read their stories, they revealed more than I was prepared to digest. I couldn't focus on the grammatical errors from being caught up in the stories. Some chose not to read their stories, as it was very painful for them to do so. At the end of the day, I got many high fives. Yes, I had touched their hearts! They were letting me in.

I went home and prayed, *Dear God what have you gotten me into? How can I help these kids get their diploma when they have so much to contend with on a*

daily basis? Dear God, I'm only one person working with twenty to thirty students.
How can I be expected to keep them on track in and out of the classroom? Dear
God, I know you did not lead me to this place to fail. Please show me a way and
give me strength. In Jesus name, Amen!

I went back to work and saw how the kids were not motivated for
many reasons. I decided to give them incentives for their achievements.
I gave away money during math speed tests. Money always seems to
motivate people. I gave away gift cards for fast food restaurants. It was
working. But how long could I keep this up? My husband warned me
not to give away all my money to these kids, and he told me not to bring
any of them home. I convinced my director to donate items to assist
with my plans. It seemed to be working, but they needed more. They
needed to get out of the dreadful place where the classes were held,
because it was not conducive to learning. Again, I went to the director
and requested funding for field trips. I was amazed at how many of
the students had never visited the Martin Luther King historical site
in downtown Atlanta. Soon we were given tickets to plays and other
local events to take the students. As all these things seemed to motivate
them, many were still dropping out for various reasons. There were
times I felt like I was in a losing battle that I had no control over.

I decided to make every Friday movie day. The catch was the students had to write a paper based on a series of questions I came up
with based on the movie. The first movie I showed them was *Freedom*
Writers. This movie was a hit with the students as they saw themselves
as the student in the movie and me as the teacher who was doing
everything to keep them on track with their studies. The next movie
I showed them was *Hotel Rwanda*. When I turned on the lights, I saw
that their eyes were full of tears. The roughest of the roughest students
showed emotions. They poured these feelings into their papers and
subsequently improved their writing skills. Things seemed to be looking better. However, this was one of many periods that was short-lived.

I came in and gave the students another writing assignment. I
wrote a quote on the board and asked them to interpret what it meant
to them. Nobody was doing the writing assignment. "I don't ask a lot
from any of you!" I said. "I expect you to come to class and put forth
your best effort. If you can't do that, then get out of my class!"

I suspended all but two students for two days. I went home frustrated. I did the only thing I knew how to do, and that was to pray.

Dear God, give me strength to do your Will. Help me reach these kids.

They returned to class, and surprisingly, they all apologized for being disrespectful. I accepted their apologies and class was back to normal. Later in the day, two male students were in a heated verbal altercation that was about to escalate into a physical altercation. I immediately ran in between the two yelling, "You will not disrespect me and the rest of the students! If you have a beef with each other, you settle it outside this class on your own time!" Before I knew it, a third student became involved. I knew I was in over my head. I had been able to defuse previous verbal altercations, but this was getting out of control. I had no regard for my safety, but was only aware of the safety of the other students. If one was carrying a weapon, somebody could get hurt. The entire class was in an uproar. "Call 911!" I yelled to a student. She in turned asked, "What is the number?"

"Just dial 9-1-1!"

While trying to separate the students, one punched a brick wall and blood was gushing from his knuckles. It was at this point I took off my heels and started shoving bodies to get them to disburse. Fear seemed to have left my body and anger had taken over. The police arrived and the two students who had started the altercation were pointed out. One officer had a warrant for his arrest and so they arrested him on the spot. The other student was ordered to leave the grounds. When I returned to the class and got the students settled, one of them said, "Yo, Mrs. J, now I believe you from the hood."

I smiled and thought, *What was I thinking?*

I went home and told my husband of the day's events. He told me to be careful and not to jeopardize my safety. I heard him loud and clear, but at the same time, I started to question my purpose for being on this job, in this position. I knew deep down inside that it was more than to help a group of kids who society had written off. There were days I just wanted to throw up my hands and say "I quit." Several people who had been in this position before me had done just that. There was an inner voice I kept hearing that would not allow me to walk away. I kept thinking, *I don't have benefits, I have a degree, and I am making less money than I could earn elsewhere.* I came to realize it wasn't about me and what I could get out of this job; it was about what I had to give, both tangibly and non-tangibly.

I returned to work and got a call from a young man who was seeking an internship position to fulfill his college requirements. I set up an interview and told him that if he wanted to work in this environment, he couldn't be thin skinned, and he would have to show up and expect the unexpected every day. I thought having a positive male role model in the class would be an asset, especially someone close in age to the students. This proved to be true over time. It was rough at first, as some of the male students tried to bypass him and not give him the same respect they would normally give me. I explained to the intern that he shouldn't take it personally, as the majority of the students had a very difficult time dealing with change and with people who were in positions of authority over them. The students slowly warmed up to him, and his presence was a breath of fresh air. Having a full-time instructor allowed me time to pursue some creative teaching methods to ensure that the students obtained their GEDs.

One day during class, we got on the subject of religion. This one of the times when I would divert from structured lessons and have open discussions. These sessions would build their confidence, right, wrong, or different. It also provided an opportunity for an alternate way of learning. At the end of the day, I asked if any of the students wanted to go to church with me on Sunday.

Two students agreed to go, one male and one female. I agreed to pick them up and return them home. The female student was apprehensive because she had been shunned in many mainstream churches she had previously attended. She was an open lesbian and displayed masculine characteristics. I told her she had nothing to worry about in my church, and both she and the other student attended Sunday service and had a wonderful time. When the pastor gave scripture references, she went right to the particular books in the Bible.

"You know the Bible?" I asked.

"Mrs. J, I grew up in the church. I might be on the wrong path, but I know the Word."

I smiled and realized I had prejudged her when I had been advocating for others not to judge them. When it came time for visitors to meet the pastor after the service, she came back and told me she felt welcomed. She was all smiles. Both students asked if I could bring them back the following Sunday. How could I say no when they were seeking something good?

When I returned to work on Monday, the two students shared their experience with the entire class. This led to much discussion again. By the end of the week, I had several students asking if they could attend church with me on Sunday. My heart was so full of joy. They were really seeking a higher power. On Sunday, I made my rounds. My mid-size SUV was full. My husband and I had to drive two cars. The students really enjoyed themselves. My lesbian student was shocked that the pastor remembered her name. As I was driving the kids back home, I asked them to give me a summary of the sermon. They did so in a very detailed manner. I made my director aware that I had been taking students to church, and she blessed the idea. Unlike a traditional state-funded school, I had an open range on what I could do to promote and improve attendance.

Although I seemed to be reaching a good majority of the students, there were always setbacks. I watched the news every morning praying I didn't see a story from the previous night that involved one of my students. My heart would race each time I heard a story of a teen being killed. *Dear God, please don't let it be one of my students* was my daily morning prayer.

One morning I thought I heard the name of one of my students that I hadn't seen for a while, but he had never given me any problems. When I arrived to work, he was absent again, and I had to call his home to inquire about his excessive absence. His sister answered the phone and said, "Mrs. Jackson, he is dead. He was driving a stolen car and running from the police when the car crashed."

My worst nightmare had come true. "Sweetie, I am so sorry. I'm so sorry. Please give my condolence to your mother. I am so sorry." I asked the intern to take over the class while I went outside to let out a big scream and to cry my heart out. I cried as I had never cried before.

"Dear God, why? Why him? You told me this is where I'm supposed to be." I went to notify the director, and she gave me a moment to get myself together. I couldn't go home because I had a classroom full of students. I came back to the class and informed the students of their classmate's death. One student asked if we could pray. Despite all the negative things they had done, they knew the power of prayer. They gave me strength.

I shared the news with my husband and he consoled me as he had on many occasions. He told me not to take it personally, but how could I not? These were my kids—the good, the bad, and the ugly. I was feeling pressure from the director to get as many kids as possible to start testing for their GED. It seemed like when I made two steps forward, I was pushed back three steps.

There was a period when the days seemed brighter. Students were passing their GED tests. Some struggled and required so much work, but they were determined. Getting to class was a challenge for some students. I asked my director for bus passes to get some of the students to class, while at the same time, I was picking up students on the side of the road on my way to work. I agreed to pick them up if they were at a designated location en route on my drive to work. Sure enough, they were there. I started to see such a positive change in these kids. They really showed interest in coming to class on a regular basis. How could I not facilitate that desire? They already had so many odds against them.

I arrived to work early one morning hoping to get some paperwork done before the students arrived. One of my young coworkers was already there with her three children, and they were all sleeping. I startled her as I woke her to ask what she was doing there. She told me that she had lost her apartment some time ago and she had been living in the center. The kids got up and went to the bathroom to wash their faces and brush their teeth.

"How long have you been living here, and who knows that you're here?" I asked with sincere concern.

She said that she had been there several months and only one other staff member knew she was living there. Soon after telling me this, she left to get on the bus to get her kids to school, and I started sobbing. This place wasn't conducive for learning; how could someone live here with her small children?

When she returned, I gave her $150.00 and said, "This is just a small something to buy food for your kids." She cried and thanked me and we began to cry together. I told her I would do whatever I could to help her.

Dear God, my heart is so heavy. I feel like I'm in a valley and not sure which direction I should go. I can't do this by myself, Lord. Please speak to me, Lord. I'm faced with so many people who are depending on me. Let me know my purpose for being here, because I feel like I'm failing.

As soon as I prayed that prayer, God spoke to me and told me that my sole purpose for being there was not just for the kids, but for the entire organization. My heart felt ten times heavier. What was I supposed to do with this organization? I promised God that I wouldn't clock out; I would not give up. I would continue to walk in the steps He had ordered for my life, no matter where those steps lead me.

As my students began to arrive, I got a call from one of the group homes informing me that one of the students would not be coming to class because he had run away from the group home, which was a violation of his probation. "Expect the unexpected," I whispered to myself.

When I returned to class, the student was there in class. I asked him where had he been, and then I informed him that the group home told me he wasn't coming to class.

He replied, "I ran away, Mrs. J, but they can't stop me from getting my education."

I called the group home to inform them that he was fine and he was in class. They told me to ensure that he stayed in class and they were sending the police to pick him up. I asked them if it was necessary to send the police, and then I returned to the classroom and informed the instructor. Class continued as usual until the police came in the front door. Someone yelled, "Five-o!" The student knew they were there for him. He got up and ran toward the back door.

"No, don't run!" I yelled when I saw the police put their hands on their weapons. "No, no, no," I pled with him. I could envision them shooting him in the back as he tried to escape. After a short run, he stopped and they handcuffed him and placed him in the patrol car. I asked if I could talk to him before they took him away and they agreed. I gave him a hug and told him it was going to be okay. He said, "I know it's going to be okay, Mrs. J. I'll be back. They are not going to stop me from getting my education."

As the patrol car drove off, I stood there thinking *this kid is going to jail, and he's only worried about his education.*

That was enough excitement for one day. It seemed like the more I prayed for these kids, the more the enemy was trying to show me that my prayers were in vain. I had a class in an uproar and a young lady living in a building not suited for humans to live in. As I was driving home, it was placed in my heart to take this young mother and her three children and give them a place to live in my home. I thought my husband was going to hit the roof when I presented him with this idea. I told him her story and her situation. I didn't know how long they would stay with us, but I knew it was what I had to.

I thank God for the most amazing and understanding husband. When he feels I am passionate about something and it's been placed on my heart by God, he is always there to support me. We call our house a house of refuge, and that is what it has been on many occasions.

At the end of the next workday, we loaded the plastic bags full of all their belongings and I took them home, showed them their rooms, and got them settled in. They were a part of our family. It had been a while since we'd had small children in our house. The boys enjoyed playing with my son. They enjoyed being kids. Our new family members caused some minor changes in our house. We had to get up a little earlier, drop my son off to school, take her two kids to school and the youngest to daycare, and then get to work. One night after we had put the kids to bed, we sat in the sunroom and I gave her a scratch-off lottery ticket worth $100.00. I told her it wasn't mine to keep. She sat there in silence for a moment, and then this young lady poured out her heart to me. She asked me why I do what I do, for her and the kids at the school. "Why do you put up with so much and get so little in return? It's not like you need this job; hell, you don't even know when payday is. So why do you keep coming back?"

"I can't quit even though there have been days when I've just wanted to walk away. You are right, it's not about the money; but it is bigger than I am. It is about being obedient to what God has planned for my life. I thought my purpose was simply to help save the kids, but I've seen how I have had an impact on everybody I've come into contact with at that organization. If I can change the life of one student, then I've fulfilled my purpose. I might be dead and gone and never see them blossom, but I know that if I plant positive seeds, at least one will blossom into something beautiful."

The students had been doing well with their testing. I continued to feel the pressure to get as many students as I could to pass their GED testing. Now it was time to set a graduation date for the fourteen students who had successfully passed. The students were excited when it came time to order their caps and gowns. Some students couldn't afford the $25.00, but we made sure everybody had a cap and gown. (Some of the money came from me; some was from grant monies.) Since these kids were nontraditional students, I requested a nontraditional graduation. We marched in to the gospel song "Order My Steps." I asked a friend from my church to do a praise dance performance. It was a very moving ceremony. During my speech, I told the parents and guardians that I had birthed no child, but God had given me so many children. I read my poem "Imagine Me" and dedicated it to all my students. It was the last positive seed I would plant into their lives.

At the end of my speech, my honor student came and presented me with a beautiful bouquet of flowers and a big hug. As I tried to pull away, he held on to me with a tight hug. We both were crying. I whispered in his ear, "I am so proud of you, and you are going to be okay. It is time for you to spread your wings and soar!" We held each other for what seemed like twenty minutes. Once we let go, everybody clapped. I said good-bye to some of the students, but said, "I'll see you soon!" to the other students who would continue in our life skills phase.

It was back to starting a new cycle with new students coming in and dropping out along the way. The program had improved in terms of the assistance we provided the students, but no matter how things seemed to improve, a new group of students presented new problems.

I found one of my female students crying uncontrollably. In between the sobs she told me she was pregnant and she was only fifteen years old. I held her and told her she was going to be okay because she was such a smart student.

"Mrs. J, I don't even know why I'm crying. Some days I'm fine and then all of a sudden I'm crying and I can't seem to stop."

"Sweetie, that's all those hormones of yours."

"How long is this going to last, Mrs. J?"

"Well, it could be the first trimester, which is the first three months. Does your mom know you're pregnant?"

"Yes, she knows, and I'm keeping the baby."

Lord, it's going to be one of those days. Everything always seems to start in the morning hours. Give me strength.

Over the next few months, I had more interns apply for internship positions. This really helped me focus on the backlog of paperwork and the case management part of my job. I didn't think some of my students were going to make it. With each cycle of interns, I always told them they couldn't be thin-skinned, they had to be firm, and they could not show fear, even when they were afraid; and last but not least, they had to show up to work every day and expect the unexpected.

Dreams to Reality

One day Jack came home and asked if I would be willing to relocate to South Africa. I said yes without hesitation. Early in our marriage, we said that if we were still together for our twentieth wedding anniversary, we wanted to return to Korea or go to South Africa. I'd had a yearning to go to Africa since I was a child. I use to tell my mother that one day I was going to Africa. Jack applied for the position and had three interviews before they offered him the job. In December 2007, I told my director of our plans, and said that our tentative departure would be sometime in March 2008. I didn't tell the students immediately. They had become so close to me, but I knew I had equipped them with the tools they needed to succeed. I was so excited and shared the information with my intern, who was now employed with the organization. I asked him to pray that my husband would get the job. He told me he didn't want me to leave and he couldn't pray that prayer with me. I was shocked. This young man and I had prayed every morning together, and now he was telling me he wouldn't be in agreement with this prayer. I told him that I thought he was being selfish and asked him to pray for God's will to be done, and he agreed.

We started on our physical exams and began taking a series of shots. My medical clearance came and Quinton's clearance was delayed, but it finally came through approved. We then got word that Jack's clearance was denied, as one of his tests indicated there was a problem with his liver. Everything was put on hold. My dreams seemed to slowly fade away. I began to think this wasn't meant to be. I did the only thing I knew how to do.

Dear God, if it's your will that we make this move to South Africa, I pray that you work it all out. You know our heart and our desires. I turn this over to you, Lord, knowing you have the last word in everything. Amen.

I drove Jack to the hospital to have a liver biopsy. It seem like it took forever for the test results to come back. I never told my job of the delay. I simply told them I didn't know the exact date of my departure. The months of April, May, and June went by without any word as to whether we were going or not. In early July of 2008, we were all cleared health wise, which meant we could begin preparing for the move. I notified my job that my last day would be July 8, as our departure was in August. I shared the news with my students, and there were so many tears. I promised to keep in touch with them and to stay informed of their progress.

On my last day, the organization gave me a going-away party. The director and assistant director spoke very highly of me. Then my intern, who I had "adopted" as a son, spoke. The tears began to flow down my face even though I had told myself that I wouldn't cry in front of my students.

One by one, the students spoke and said some of the most moving things: "Mrs. J, you are the only woman I know that can cuss and make it sound cute...Mrs. J, thank you for saving my life...Mrs. J, thank you for being like a mom to me...Mrs. J, thank you for picking me up and bringing me to school...Thank you for caring, Mrs. J; even though you suspended me so many times I know you were doing it to make me a better person...Mrs. J, I hope you find some kids to help in Africa like you helped us."

By this time, I needed a box of tissues.

It was at that moment when I realized the impact I'd had on these kids. They really loved me in spite of the good, the bad, and the ugly days we'd had.

I tried to get myself together before I addressed the group. I looked out and saw all the tears from the students and staff members. "Wow, this has been the most gratifying moment and the most gratifying job I've had thus far. You have all made me a better person. You have all taught me many things. It has been an honor and a pleasure working with the staff and working for my kids. I will be back in two years, and I hope to hear great things about all of you. Make me proud and continue to walk in the steps that have been ordered for your lives. I love you all."

I had thirty days to have the movers come and get things in order with our house. This was a stressful time. I also needed to go see my brother before I departed. I promised him I would visit him before I left for South Africa. I made the long drive to Florida alone. Every time I went to visit him, I felt like I was walking down death row. This time was no different, but we had a nice visit, and I left a little early because it was such a long drive back to Atlanta.

We continued to move forward with our move. The house, our cars, and our dog were taken care of. We were ready. After all the little bumps and medical scares, we departed Atlanta, Georgia on 08-08-08. As the airplane took off, I thought how wonderful it was that we were starting a new life on that day. The number eight represents new beginnings and prosperity. Here we were leaving on a day of triple eights, one for each of us. South Africa, here we come!

On August 9, 2008, I heard the same announcement I used to day-dream about in school back in Bridgeport, Connecticut: "Ladies and gentlemen, welcome to Johannesburg, South Africa. On behalf of our airline, we hope you enjoy your stay."

I had arrived at the place I'd longed for and dreamt of soften throughout my life. I was really here! After an eighteen-hour flight, we disembarked the plane. I took a deep inhale of breath and noticed that the air seemed different. As we made our way through baggage claim and customs, I was smiling from ear to ear. I had no idea who or what awaited us behind the sliding glass doors as we exited the secure area, but we were welcomed by one of Jack's colleagues. We quickly made our way outside the airport, and I wanted to drop down and kiss the ground. I felt like a kid in a candy store. I couldn't believe I was really in Africa. There wasn't much to see as we arrived in the evening and it was getting dark.

We had left Atlanta, Georgia in ninety-degree temperatures and arrived in South Africa where it was a lot cooler. The first of many adjustments was getting accustomed to living in the Southern Hemi-sphere. We arrived at a big two-story house. The caretaker met us there and introduced us to our temporary home. There was no heat-ing system. We only had portable heaters in each bedroom and in the living room area. She gave us a quick lesson on the intercom system and the remote for the gate. Jack's colleague took us out to dinner and returned us to this beautiful house with all antique furnishings. My cell phone was still active, so we called family members to let them know we had arrived safe and sound. We showered then watched a little TV once we figured out how to operate the remote. It was 9:00 p.m., but we weren't really tired as our bodies were still on Atlanta time as though it was only 3:00 p.m. We finally settled down as we had an early start in the morning.

I woke up early to have my coffee and have a good look at everything we couldn't see in the dark the night before. Our house was surrounded by four seven-foot walls with electric wires on top of them. *Good Lord, I feel like I'm in prison.* I could hear cars going by but I couldn't see anything on the other side of the massive concrete wall. The property grounds were beautiful and well-manicured.

The driver arrived and we started our day by going to the school to finish the enrollment process for Quinton who was starting school in two days. I was taking in all the sights as we drove down the highway. When we exited the highway, we saw a large shantytown alongside the road. "People really live there?" I asked the driver. How could anybody live in those conditions? There seemed to be hundreds of tiny tin houses cramped so close to one another. People were moving around and walking everywhere, but where were they going? They looked like ants just wandering around. I prayed silently, *Thank you, Jesus, for blessing me.*

The school campus was a huge fifty-seven acres—one hundred times bigger than the small Christian academy Quinton had attended in Atlanta. Everything was complete and his paperwork was sorted out. The driver took a different route when bringing us back home. There was so much open land. Although the landscape looked dry, it still was so beautiful. We returned to the prison of a house and walked to the grocery store. Trying to cross the street was a challenge. I hadn't become accustomed to cars driving on the left side of the road. We walked up and down the aisles in the store, trying to decide what to buy. It was a challenge because none of the brands seemed familiar. My first Coke in South Africa had a different taste to it. I decided to make chicken, and even the chicken had a fresh game taste to it.

We settled into the living room to watch TV, but there were only three channels, and they were speaking an African language. We decided to watch a movie on the laptop computer. Ironically, we had brought this movie with us, and it was about homeless boys in South Africa. We had been warned about the high crime rate prior to our arrival. The movie helped us understand a little about why there were walls around all the houses.

The next morning Quinton was ready for school. There are no bus stops like in the States. The bus picks up and drops off each child in front of his or her home. As I was sitting in the backyard, drinking my coffee and letting the dog out, a lady appeared out of nowhere. She startled me as she came over to introduce herself.

"Hello, I'm Namsa."

"Good morning. Where did you come from?" I asked. She motioned to the side of the garage. We chatted for a moment then a young girl bought her a cup of tea. She introduced her. "This is my daughter Precious, and I have another daughter, Beyoncé."

"It is nice to meet you, Namsa. We will chat later."

"Ma'am, do you need a cleaning lady?"

"No, they will send someone to clean the house."

"When you move to your house, I can clean and iron for you."

"I don't think I'll need anybody to do that, but thank you for asking. Give me your number and if I change my mind, I will call you."

We spent one week in the temporary house. Our new home for the next two years was nothing like the home we left in Georgia. We went from a tri-level home with over 4500 square feet to a very small ranch house. The master bedroom was the size of the sitting area in my master bedroom in Georgia. Everything was much smaller, but we couldn't complain since it was a government house, and we didn't have to pay for anything; rent, utilities, furniture, water—all of it was paid for us. The good thing about this new home was that it had heat.

Living in a smaller house wasn't as challenging as crossing the streets and learning to drive on the opposite side of the road and having the driver's side on the opposite side of the car. My first driving experience was a little frightening. I came to a roundabout (circle) and couldn't figure out where to get off. To make things worse, I was driving a car with manual transmission and trying to talk to Jack on the cell phone for directions. I just kept going around and around. I avoided known roundabouts until we had a car with automatic transmission, which made it easier.

We got settled into what was to be our home for the next two years. In October, the shipment with our belongings finally arrived. It was good to see familiar things again. In a matter of time, we had satellite TV and Internet. With the Internet, I was not only able to surf the web, but it allowed us to talk to our family and friends back in the United States while keeping our stateside phone number.

My sponsor came by to see how things were going. She informed me about a position and asked if I had plans to work. I said, "I'm not the stay at home mom/wife type, but I don't plan on working until we are completely settled in and I've had a chance to adjust to everything."

"Well, there is a position that's open, and the supervisor is a nice down-to-earth lady," she reassured me.

"Okay, I'll apply as soon as our printer arrives. It's in our other shipment that hasn't arrived yet." She informed me that the job would be closed by then and I could use her computer and printer.

I applied for a position with the United States Secret Service. As I waited for my background and security clearance to be completed, I worked as a temporary hire in human resource.

In March 2009, I was granted my clearance to begin working for the United States Secret Service. My days were long as I was introduced to a whole new world and learning things faster than I could comprehend. As I came home tired each day, I thought about Namsa, the lady I had met in the backyard of the temporary house. I questioned several people about their experiences with housekeepers. I was told that everybody had a domestic, and that it was almost an insult not to have one. I found my journal where I had written Namsa's name and number. I called her and asked if she was still interested in working for me, and if so, if she was available for an interview. We met on a Saturday, and I told her that I only needed someone three days a week as the house was small and it was primarily just my son and me, as my husband traveled a lot.

When we met, she was very humble and passive. She never made eye contact with me the entire time we talked. I assumed she was very shy. After we agreed on the fee, her work schedule, and her duties, I drew up a contract and told her she could start the following week.

She said, "Ma'am, my husband is a gardener, and he is looking for a piece job."

"What is a piece job?" I asked.

"He can come maybe one or two days a week," she explained.

"Oh, a part time job," I said, realizing what she meant. "Okay, I'll speak to my husband about it, and I will let you know."

I started each morning by taking the dog out for a walk. There were a lot of people out doing the same, but nobody spoke or said good morning. After several weeks, it hit me: *They must think I'm the hired help*. There were no other blacks on our street. Everybody stayed closed up behind the walls and electric fences surround their houses. The next day, I started out on my walk determined to speak to a few people. "Good morning," I said to each one who passed by. Surprisingly, people started to greet me after that. Each day more and more initiated a greeting. I suddenly realized that they had heard my accent and realized I was not a black South African but an American.

I didn't understand why it was okay to speak to me as an American but not if I was a South African. Even when I went shopping, whites were very accommodating and eager to assist once they heard my voice. It made me angry as a black person because I am no different from the black South Africans, and not all black South Africans are domestic workers. I guess I could accept that it is what it is, but I couldn't. I didn't know my role, nor did I understand the race relations in South Africa. I couldn't believe the classism that is a part of society there, and how it relates to the various categories of races. It definitely plays a role in how one is treated by others. As I befriended people of various races, I tried to understand the race relations of this country from each person's perspective. Amazingly, each gave a good argument for why things are the way they are even after apartheid. What I found more amazing is that each group is represented at the US Embassy, and they all work side by side together. However, if I had to sum it up, I would say that they tolerate each other, but they do not socialize outside the workplace. I can easily have lunch in the mall with each group, but I never see them interacting with one another. I'm reminded that it's because I'm an American.

Dear God, help me to understand my role and my purpose for being in this place. There are obvious wounds that I can't heal. I know you have purpose for my life here. Please give me wisdom and knowledge to know and understand my role. There are so many people in need in this beautiful country, and there are so many open wounds. Help me discern as I continue to walk in the steps you've ordered for my life. In Jesus name I pray, Amen.

I became intrigued about the race relations of this country. It felt as though I was living in the late 1960s or early 1970s in the United States. I found that black South Africans were the most complex group of people. Some admired the fact that I'm an American, and there was a sense of hope when talking with them. However, on the opposite end of the spectrum, I found that some resented me. The main subject of my interactions with black South Africans was my hair. Some wanted to know if it was a weave while others asked what was wrong with letting my hair be in its natural state. Some suggested I was a coconut: brown on the outside and white on the inside.

I got into a heated debate with a black South African about our differences. I was made to feel like I had forgotten who I was as a black woman. I became very defensive and stated that I could not apologize for my ancestors being taken from Africa to America. Truth be told, I think black Americans were treated worse than any group of people. We were stripped of our names, our customs, our traditions, and our heritage.

"I will not apologize for being African American," I said to one South African, who then asked me, "What does it mean when you say you're African American? You are not from Africa; you are simply an American."

I learned that most black Africans do not see me as an extension of them but simply as an American. I found this to be very contradictive when I was referred to as "sissy" or "my sista" on a regular basis. I learned to accept it for what it is. This was not my battle, nor was I going to make a difference in the deeply ingrained perceptions of many.

Dear God, please show me my purpose for being here. There are so many in need in every conceivable way. What is my role in this place? I'm patiently waiting to hear from you.

As time went on, I began to notice a certain young kid who was always at the traffic light begging. He was just one of many in South Africa. However, this kid captured my heart for some reason. I would give him my change from time to time. I could be several blocks away and he would spring to life when he saw my car coming down the street. One day I decided to get out of the car and talk to him. He told me his name. I asked him how old was he and how he had ended up on the streets begging. He told me that his mother had died, and he had never known his father. He had been raised by his grandmother until one day at the age of twelve he came home and everything was gone, including her. When he asked the neighbors in the township what had happened, he was told that she had left. Ever since then he had been on the streets trying to survive. I told him to get into the car and I was taking him to get some food from the grocery store. As we walked back to the car, I told him, "Don't ever take my kindness as a weakness, and if I ever find out you're using my money for drugs or anything like that, I'm going to whip your ass. Do you understand what I mean by whipping your ass?"

"Yes, Mommy," he replied. "You are going to beat me."

"Right!"

I saw him every day at the same intersection whenever I went by the embassy. He had the most amazing smile that would light up any-body's heart. I came home one day and told my son to gather up all the clothes he had outgrown. I returned to give the boy the bag of clothes. I told him I had better see him with the clothes on, and that he was *not* to sell them.

"Okay, Mama," he said.

Mama—I now had another child I did not birth. This fourteen-year-old kid had such an impact on me. I loved his spirit and his smile. There were days I'd run him off the streets and tell him I didn't want to see him there later in the day because I had given him more money than he could make in a week. I would make my rounds just to see if he would be there. To my surprise, he wasn't, but then I wondered where he went when it was raining outside. I wanted to take a camera and follow him around just to see life from his perspective, but neither time nor my job would allow me to do that.

In August 2009, we were preparing to return to the United States for Jack's oldest son's wedding in early September. I kept getting calls from my mother informing me that my brother's health was deteriorating. I felt that all I could do was to pray for him. Three days prior to our departure I talked with the hospital staff that told me my brother's bone marrow cancer had gotten worse and he only had weeks to live, if that left.

Dear God, please be with my brother. Please ease his pain and heal his body. Touch his body and let him know you are still God and anything is possible. Let him confess his sins and allow you to come into his heart. In Jesus name I pray, Amen.

After praying for my brother, I told Jack that I needed to go home to visit my brother. If he was in fact as sick as I'd been told, then I needed to see him. I quickly changed my flight to depart earlier than I had planned and fly to Florida. The prison granted me special provision to see him on an off-visitation day. I arrived in Florida on a Wednesday evening after a long twenty-hour flight only to wake up the next morning at 4:00 a.m. to start the four-hour drive to the prison. *Dear God give me strength.*

My mother made the drive with me, and when we arrived at the prison, we had to wait a bit longer than usual in the visitation area. It took a while for my brother to come down to see us, as he was not expecting any visitors. I anxiously waited for him to walk through the door. When the door opened, I saw a guard pushing him in a wheelchair. The tears started to flow from both of us.

"Awww, man, my bougie sister is here to see me. Man, Terran, words can't express what a surprise this is to see you. You came all the way from Africa to see me?"

As we embarrassed, I could feel every vertebra in his back. He was so skinny. He asked me not to squeeze to tight as he was in a lot of pain. He couldn't stand up. We just held hands and looked into each other's eyes. I could clearly see his pain as much as he was trying to be so strong. We did our usual routine of ordering food, but this time he didn't eat half as much as he used to.

My mother left us to have a moment alone with each other. I told him so many people were praying for him. He said he knew because he could feel it. "I know God has been watching over me. They initially gave me eighteen months to live and now I'm at month twenty-two. Yo sis, I want you to know I am so proud of you and all that you have accomplished. I'm so grateful for you watching over my seeds for all the years I've been away."

I choked back the tears and said, "I've done what I could for all of them. I promised you I would, and I've never gone back on that promise."

"Girly, you don't know how proud I am to call you my sister. You made it from the project to Pretoria, South Africa working for the United States Secret Service. How dope is that?"

I just smiled in a response and waited for him to speak again.

"Yo, how is the book coming? Have you decided on a title yet?"

"The book is a work in progress. I've chosen one of the titles you suggested—Wisdom While Walking—and I'm dedicating it to you."

Our time was ending soon, and he had a request for me and made me promise to relay his message. "Sis, everybody got this whole thing wrong. I'm not a bad person. I'm not the monster they say I am. Please tell them I'm not a bad person. I'm not a bad person, sis."

"I know you're not a bad person, Byron. I will tell them."

This was my brother's way of telling me that this would be the last time I would see him alive. He told me he had made his peace with God and he was good and not to worry about him. How could I not worry about him? He was my only brother, the one I had watched after in our younger years. We only had a half hour left for our visit, and he must have seen how tired and weak I was feeling, despite how bad he probably felt too. "It's okay to go now," he said. "I know you been on a long journey, and you still have to drive back home. Take Ma Dukes back home, and y'all drive back safely; a storm is coming."

"Okay, I love you so much. Thank you for the book title. Thank you for being my brother. I love you so much."

As we departed the facility, it started to rain. My stomach was in knots. As much as I wanted to drop to my knees and cry, I couldn't let my mother see me shaken. I'm the oldest and I'm expected to be strong even in the middle of a storm. The drive was silent. I knew that if I started to talk, I would break down. I wanted to pull over on the side of the road and throw up. I knew in my heart that I wouldn't see my brother alive again. The storm got worse. I was so tired that I could hardly focus on the road, and the car was swerving from side to side. I could only drive twenty miles an hour. I couldn't see anything in front of me. My mother kept asking was I okay to drive. I prayed, *Dear God, I need you right now. Please calm the storm. Cover us, dear God.* As I prayed, my mind was brought back to a story a friend had sent me in an email. A father and daughter were driving through a storm and the daughter kept asking the father why he wouldn't pull over to wait for the storm to pass. The father kept insisting that he was going to press his way through even though the highway was lined with cars that had pulled off the road. Finally, after making it through the storm, the father looked in the rearview mirror and saw that the storm was now behind them. He told his daughter to look back and think about all those people who were still in the storm because they had stopped. He then said sometimes you have to keep going and press your way through the storm. As they drove on and the clouds parted to reveal a clear blue sky, he said, "We're in the clear sunshine again, while they are still in the storm.

I was so thankful that God had reminded me of that story just when I needed it. *Dear God, thank you for bringing this back to my memory,* I prayed, and I pressed on.

We made it back to my mother's house safe and sound. I was running out of time. The storm had slowed me down so much that I didn't have time to visit with any family members. I had to get up at 4:00 a.m. the next morning for a 6:00 a.m. flight to Washington, DC for Jack's son's wedding.

The wedding was beautiful, but my thoughts were still in Florida. I found myself crying at different times, but I was crying for my brother. I told Jack that I didn't know if I would see my brother alive again, and I was so glad that I had gone to visit him. I really tried to focus on the wedding and the happy event. It was a beautiful wedding. The fact that they got married on Jack's birthday made the event even more special.

Now it was time to make the long flight back to South Africa. I arrived back to work on September 9 and poured myself into my work as I was preparing for a major inspection. My mother called to give me updates on my brother's health. My sisters, nieces, and nephews went to visit him, as he was asking to see everybody he could see. Everybody had a good visit with him, and he always seemed to be in good spirits despite the pain he was experiencing.

September 18, 2009, I was on the phone with my mother when another call came in. I looked at the caller ID and it read Florida State Prison. I told my mother to hold on.

When I took the other call, a voice said, "Hello this is the chaplain from Florida State Prison. I'm trying to reach Terran Jackson, sister of inmate Byron Bryant."

"Yes, this is she."

"Mrs. Jackson, it is with great regret that I'm calling you to inform you that Byron passed last night."

I let out the loudest scream. "No…no…no!" Then realizing I had screamed in the chaplain's ear, I said, "I'm so sorry, sir, I'm so sorry. Oh my God, no!"

"Ma'am, I am sorry for your loss. I tried to reach your mother and the number is not working. I was unable to reach his wife in Germany. He had you listed as his sister with your contact details. I'm sorry, ma'am, but I couldn't reach anybody else. Is there anybody else you want us to contact?"

"No, no, you did the right thing; I was just on the phone with my mother. I have to tell her myself. Sir, I'm in South Africa. What has to be done to bring his body home to South Florida, and how soon can we have this arranged?"

"By state law, every inmate must undergo an autopsy. His body should be ready for release in two days, and you can arrange for the funeral home of your choice to pick up his body."

Pick up his body? I couldn't believe what I was hearing. I was in a state of shock, even though I had tried to prepare myself for this moment. I managed to get myself together and thanked the chaplain for calling. I sat on the floor and wept uncontrollably. Jack just held me, trying to console me. During this whole time, my mother was calling in on the other line. I pleaded with Jack not to answer the phone. "No, Jack, not yet. I can't tell her yet. Please let me get myself together first. Please, please…I will call her back in a minute. Dear God, how am I going to tell my mother her only son is dead?"

It had been several minutes since I'd spoken with the chaplain, but in my head I kept hearing *your brother passed last night.* I couldn't break this news without somebody being there with my mother. I first called my aunt, but she didn't answer the phone. I then called my brother's first wife and broke the news to her, and I pleaded with her to have somebody go to my mother's house. My mother was still calling me and I couldn't take her call until I knew she had someone there to support her. My sister-in-law informed me that my niece was at the house with my mother.

I called my mother, and she was already crying and screaming in the phone. She knew that the news wasn't good when I did not come back to the phone and didn't answer my phone.

She kept wailing, "Is he gone? Is he gone? No, no…don't tell me he's gone…please don't tell me he's gone."

"I'm so sorry, Ma. Byron is gone."

"When did he die?"

"The chaplain said he passed last night in his sleep and the nurse found him. It's going to be okay, Ma. He's not suffering anymore. He has gone to a better place."

"Byron, Byron, my baby boy! Oh, God, no!"

I didn't know what to feel. I was so far away, and all I wanted was to hold my mother and console her. I told my mother I would call her back. I called my sister, and my niece answered the phone crying. I could hear my sister in the background wailing uncontrollably. I couldn't talk to her either. My thoughts were in a whirl. *My God, this family has fallen apart and I can't talk to anybody.* I called my oldest nephew and broke the news to him, and then I asked him to go be with his grandmother and sister. I made phone calls to inform several of our friends and family members that Byron had passed. My mind was racing and I was in autopilot mode. I'm the oldest and I had to make sure things were taken care of even though I was worlds apart from everybody.

After a few hours, I called my mother back. We both were a little bit calmer and were able to speak of the inevitable arrangements. I told her to contact the funeral home and see if we could get the service for the upcoming Saturday. I told her I would be flying out on Wednesday and would arrive in the States on Thursday. We could have the wake on Friday and the funeral on Saturday.

I went to work on Monday and informed my supervisor of my brother's passing and my plans of going home. There was such support from my coworkers. They were my extended family, and they were with me every step. I felt like being at work because it kept my mind busy. If I were at home, I would find myself crying all day, and there was nothing for me to do at home; and because of the time difference, I couldn't speak to my mother during the day anyway.

Everything was set into motion. I was returning to the States alone because I didn't want to take Quinton out of school. Jack stayed behind with him. My body was so tired because I went to work every day and didn't sleep much during the night. I arrived in Florida after twenty hours of flying. I still couldn't rest as I hit the ground trying to assist my mother with the final preparations. All nine of my brother's children were there. My sister arrived from Georgia. As a family, our first stop was to meet with the florist to pick out flowers. Everybody had an opinion and nobody had money to contribute. I took everyone's input and made the final decision.

The next stop was more difficult. We went to buy a suit for my brother. We piled into several cars and went shopping for a suit. As much as I wanted to break down, I couldn't. I picked out a beautiful brown suit, a shirt, and a tie. When we went outside, my sister from Georgia was at the other end of the parking lot walking around in circles sobbing. This was the first of many dramatic moments I wasn't going to tolerate. "Wanda, get in the car. We have to get this stuff to the funeral director before a certain time and we don't have time for this. Get yourself together and let's go!" She got into one of the cars and we drove off.

We got everything to the funeral director, but not in time for us to view my brother before the wake on Friday. We still had to make sure all the kids and grandkids had appropriate clothing for the funeral. I had brought extra clothes and lent a dress suit to a niece and some pants and shirts to my nephew's sons. Everyone was to wear black or white, or some combination of the two. My youngest sister chose not to wear a dress but pants. I think my mother really wanted her in a dress but did not press the issue. Everything was settled and we were all ready for the wake the next day.

Family members arrived from out of town. I was so exhausted. I hadn't slept in three days. My nephews had ordered T-shirts to wear after the funeral in memory of my brother. They chose a nice picture. However, when I read the shirt, I immediately spotted some misspelled words. "This is why it pays to stay in school," I stated. Nevertheless, we all ordered the shirts. My sister Wanda asked me to place the order for her and her family. I agreed as long as she was to give me the money back. She already owed me a thousand dollars from when I assisted her move to Georgia the previous year. I told her bluntly, "Wanda, I want my money when I deliver the shirts. If you don't have the money, then you don't get the shirts." My sister-in-law and I went down to pick up the order, and when I returned, my sister only had part of the money. I held the shirts until she gave me the balance of what she owed me.

That night I stayed at my aunt's house, as my mother's house was full of family members. It was the first time I rested. My body had no choice but to sleep. I woke up Friday morning at the break of dawn and took a drive on the beach. Every time I'm home, I drive on the beach each morning. It is the one place where I can always find peace. As I sat on the beach with a cup of coffee, reality hit me. I was there to bury my only brother. In a few hours, I would see his body in a casket. My eyes started to swell with tears. I had been so busy for the past five days that I hadn't really allowed myself time to cry and grieve. I also didn't want to break down in front of my mother.

I went to my mother's house and spent the day with family members and friends. Then, it was time: time for us to go to the wake. My mother started to break down as we were gathering to get into the cars. I prayed silently, *Dear God, please give me strength in the name of Jesus.* We finally got her in the car and arrived at the funeral home. Everybody was there except one of my nephews, my brother's namesake. Nobody could reach him, as he wasn't answering his phone. Once again, I had to take charge. "We can't continue to wait. We have to view Byron's body before people start to arrive," I stated firmly.

Just when I thought we were ready, my mother would not get out of the car. "I can't do it! I can't…I can't…" she kept saying.

"Ma, you can do this; you have to do this. Catch your breath before you make yourself sick. We're all here with you, and we are going to make it through this as a family."

We managed to get her out of the car and into her wheelchair. The closer we got to the entrance of the funeral home, the louder she cried. I instructed my sister to wheel her inside. My heart was racing so fast that I thought it was going to jump out of my chest as we gathered and waited in the lobby. I went to each of my nieces and nephews and told them, "We're going to be okay; we've just got to be strong."

I pulled my mother's wheelchair in front of the chapel doors and took a deep breath, and then I nodded to the director to signal that we were ready. As he opened the doors, I could see my brother's body lying in the casket at the front of the chapel. There was an outburst of screaming and crying as the others caught sight of him. I led the way down the aisle while pushing my mother. The tears I had been holding back began to flow. I couldn't cry out as much as I wanted to. There we were standing in front of the casket with my brother in it. He had lost even more weight from when I had last seen him three weeks prior.

My mother gestured for us to help her stand up. We pulled her to a standing position and she braced herself on the side of the casket. "My baby…my only boy," she said as she rubbed his head and gently leaned down to kiss his forehead. We assisted her back to her wheelchair. All his kids stood there sobbing. We were still missing BJ and wondering why he wasn't there. We all took turns standing there giving our respect.

We gave the funeral director the okay to allow visitors in, as we had regained our composure. As friends and family members came in, the tears started to flow again. There were family members I hadn't seen in years. Then my tears turned to anger as an unwanted visitor entered the door: the man that was believed to have sent my brother to death row. As I stood to confront him, my nieces, nephews, and mother begged me not to say anything to him. I promised I wouldn't unless he came off wrong. He came and paid his respects to my mother, and then he kept moving. As I watched him walk out the door, I saw my nephew BJ coming through the door. I whispered in my mother's ear that BJ had made it. Everybody made way and let him give his respects alone. He then turned to my mother and broke down on her shoulder. This sent another wave of emotions through the room because everybody knew how much Byron Junior loved his father.

After a few hours, I told my mother it was time to go and she agreed. We all returned to her place and sat around reminiscing about our childhood days and telling stories of my brother that his children had never heard. I told my mother I was going to get some rest and I would see them in the morning. I returned to my aunt's house, but before getting out of the car, I sat in the driveway and just cried and cried. My heart was so full and heavy. I was angry because I'd been carrying the whole load for everyone, it seemed, and my father wasn't there because he was serving a twelve-year prison sentence for arson. Although my mother had insurance on my brother, there was still an outstanding balance with the funeral home. I had asked my sister Wanda if she could help me pay the remainder of that bill, and she had said she would try to give me something.

A heavy burden was on my shoulders. I called my mother and told her how I was feeling. I told her I just get tired of being the go-to person all the time. "I'm just tired, Ma. I can't keep doing this all by myself. I paid for my flight, rented a car, and paid for the suit and flowers without anybody saying 'here is a dollar to help.'" She said she understood.

Saturday morning came quickly. Everybody was to meet at my aunt's house for the lineup. My cousin said the prayer before we got into the cars headed for the funeral, which was being held at the church. When the limo pulled up for the immediate family members, my mother again refused to get into the car. I had attended many funerals, but had never ridden in the family car. The ride to the church seemed like the longest ride of my life. It was so hot and the air conditioner in the car didn't seem to be working.

We arrived at the church and my heart was racing fast again. *Dear God, help me to keep it together.* I lined up all my brother's children behind my mother, my sisters, and me. I thought the funeral wouldn't be so bad as we had just seen his body the night before, but a wave of emotions flowed through my body as we walked down the aisle while the choir was singing. One by one, we took turns at the casket to say our good-byes, and then they closed the casket. I heard screaming from all over the church. It was final—I would never see my brother again. I would never read another letter from him. I would never hear his voice again. I focused on my mother and tried to keep her calm. I told her he was now in a better place and the state of Florida did not have the chance to take his life.

People came forward to speak about my brother. Then it was my turn.

"My brother Byron Bernard Bryant (B-Bop) had a smile that could light up any room. His laughter was addictive and mesmerizing at the same time. He was charming and very charismatic. For a man who did not complete high school, he was very articulate and deliberate with his words. He could research and debate on any subject. His mind was sharp and he could give you very vivid details of people, places and things that had long been forgotten by others. He lived vicariously through others….he's been to Africa, Asia, Europe, South America and seen the many changes of his beloved Delray…. He was an intel-lectual man who thought deep thoughts. They caged his body but not his mind.…..I sent him excerpts from the transcripts for a book I've been working on I told him that I didn't have a title….maybe it would come to me when it was all done….. In his next letter to me, he sent several titles without me asking… One in particular hit me like a ton of bricks and I told him I was going to use it and dedicate it to him for the title……Wisdom While Walking. Yes he was a gifted man! On many occasions he asked me to do things for him…if I could, I would, if I couldn't I would let him know. During my last visit 3 weeks ago, he stated "I'm not a bad person." Before I walked away he told me, tell them I'm not a bad person. So today I tell you Byron was not a bad person."

After I returned to my seat, my mother requested that they open the casket one more time before we departed for the cemetery, and the funeral directors agreed. They opened the casket and rolled it down to the front pew where the family was seated so that we could say a final goodbye. They started on the end of the pew opposite to where my mother and I were seated. I was leaning in toward my mother when somebody tapped me on the shoulder and motioned for me to get my youngest sister's attention. I looked down the pew and saw my sister pulling the casket toward her as the funeral personnel were trying to move it in the opposite direction.

My mother asked what was going on, as her sight was gone from diabetes. I whispered, "Tanya's down there playing tug-of-war with the casket, and she won't let go." My mother asked me to go talk to my sister. I got up and walked around to where Tanya was seated, and I tried to talk to her and comfort her, but to no avail. My cousin came to assist as things were getting out of control. As I was talking to Tanya, Wanda got a hold on the casket and was almost inside the casket. There was a loud scream and crying from all over. I prayed frantically, *Dear God, help me!* I looked at my mother, who was sitting there not really knowing what was going on in all this confusion. After I managed to get everybody back to their seats, I didn't get the chance to see my brother again. As soon as I made my way back to my mother's side, I couldn't sit down. I looked down the bench and saw my sister Wanda laid out. If I hadn't been in church, I probably would have said a few cuss words. I went to Wanda and pulled her upright, and told her husband to make her sit up and stop this foolishness as she was making it worse for my mother.

The service had ended and all my nephews were the pallbearers for their father. I was so proud of them. We made our way to the cemetery, and my mother's wheelchair couldn't make it through the sand, so we parked her at the head. We were all given a flower to put on Byron's casket as we walked by. After I placed my flower on the casket and proceeded to my seat, I saw the casket rolling forward almost coming off the belts that were holding it up. I turned and saw that Wanda had collapsed her body on the casket and was pushing it forward. "Oh, my God," I said, and kept walking. After the service, it was time to get back in the car. Wanda was falling out and her husband was trying to get her to the car. I'd had enough of the drama. I was tired and hot and I wasn't in the mood for all the craziness. "Get her in this car or she will be left right out here at this cemetery. It's too hot out here for all this foolishness!" Thankfully, he got her under control and into the car. We all changed into our T-shirts and met back at the church for the repast, and then we went back to my mother's house where we shared more stories. We gave my mother a recap of what had transpired at the funeral, as she wasn't able to see what was going on. We laughed and joked with each other. It was like the old days. My mother got her wish but for the wrong reasons. She had wished for many years that all four of her children could be together at one time. Although the occasion was a somber one, we were all together in the same room for a brief moment.

Later that evening my sister and her husband left to go on the casino boat. I asked her if she was going to be able to assist me in the remaining balance that was left from my brother's funeral, and she told me she didn't have it. I was so upset because once again, I was expected to take care of everything. I told my mother I didn't expect anything from her because she had made the payments for my brother's insurance. My mother asked what my sister had said about helping me. "She said she doesn't have no money. She better have some damn life insurance when she dies." I left my mother's house in anger. I met with the funeral director and paid the remaining balance prior to my departure.

I woke up early in the morning to visit my brother's grave before I headed back to South Africa. I told him I love him and to be at peace. I then made my last trip to the beach. I was so tired from lack of sleep and the emotional rollercoaster ride of anger and sadness I'd been on since arriving here. I said my goodbyes to everybody and made my way to the airport. As I gazed out the window, I was reminded of why I had made this long journey. I prayed and asked God to give me peace. I flew from Florida to Georgia. I checked in and made some calls to people I hadn't had a chance to see before moving to South Africa. I was on the phone with my girlfriend when I heard my name being called on an intercom in the airport. I told her I would call her back as they were calling me to the check-in desk. The attendant asked for my boarding pass, passport, and ticket. I told her I had already checked in. She stated she was issuing me a new seat. As they called for boarding, I got on the plane and realized I was sitting in first class. I asked an attendant if this was the correct seat, and she said yes. I didn't realize they had upgraded me to first class.

As I was calling my girlfriend back, an attendant came and asked if I wanted champagne or orange juice. I told my girlfriend, "Girl, how 'bout the reason they were calling me to the counter was because they changed my ticket to first class. I think God was looking at me and said 'my poor child, I will give you rest'. *How cool is this?* I thought. I didn't know how to operate anything in my little cubicle. After taking off, I realized the seat opened out into a full flat bed. I had a real feather pillow along with all the other little gifts they give you in first class. When it came time for dinner, I had real silverware, not the plastic stuff. The attendants were very nice and attentive. I went into the bathroom and found it to be twice the size of the economy bathroom. I could turn around in it and still had room to move around. *Dear God, thank you! You must have seen how tired your child was.* When I returned to my seat, I started to watch a movie and only made it halfway through. I slept the entire flight. When I woke up, the first thing I did was look at my legs to see if they were swollen as they usually are on long flights, but they were fine, and my back wasn't aching, either. I was so refreshed. I was all smiles when I departed the airport.

I arrived in South Africa on Friday and went back to work on Monday, October 3, 2009. I gave my supervisor details of all that had transpired at home during the funeral. We laughed when I told her about my sisters, and she said, "You just can't make this stuff up!" She also reminded me that to whom much is given much is required. I poured myself into my work because we were getting ready for a major office inspection.

On October 5, 2009 at 3:00 a.m., my stateside phone was ringing. *This is too early for it to be anything good,* I thought. I ignored it the first few times thinking it was solicitors calling, but it kept ringing. Jack woke up and said it must be an emergency for somebody to call so many times. I got up and looked at the caller ID. Each call was from my mother's cell phone. *Dear God, don't tell me somebody is calling to tell me my mother has passed.* I called my mother's number and she answered the phone. *Thank God she is okay* were my first thoughts until I heard her crying as she was trying to get the words out of her mouth. "She's gone, she's gone. Wanda is gone!"

"What do you mean, she's gone? Has she left her husband and kids? What do you mean?"

"Wanda had a heart attack at work and she's dead."

Once again, I felt like I was dreaming and my mother was making a mistake. We had just been together a few days ago. How could this be possible? My mother hung up the phone, as she was so distraught. Jack had come into the living room to console me. "Wanda is dead!" I cried out, and fell into his arms.

I got myself together and phoned my mother again. I told her I would be there as soon as possible. I sat up trying to make sense of the news I had been given. The first thing that came to mind was the argument I'd had with Wanda about the money she owed me, and me stating to my mother that Wanda better have life insurance when she died.

I called my supervisor to tell her I would be late because I had just gotten the news of my sister's death. It had only been a few days before when I was telling her how my sister had acted up at my brother's funeral, and now she was dead. Once again, I asked God to give me strength to help my family through yet another trying time. After a few hours, I went to work. I couldn't see myself staying at home. I was physically at work, but mentally I was in another world. I tried to keep myself busy, but I kept breaking down. I made it through the day, and when I came home, I called my mother to ask about funeral arrangements. As difficult as it was, I had to know. She told me my sister had requested to be cremated and have her ashes scattered in the Atlantic Ocean. I asked my mother when she wanted to have the funeral. Since my sister didn't have any life insurance, we were dealing with having her body moved from Georgia to Florida. The community gave money to my sister's kids, and that paid for her body to be sent home.

The next challenge was to get my nieces, nephew, and my sister Tanya back to Florida. Although Wanda was married, her husband did not contribute anything to assist us. I was so far away, and trying to organize things from afar was very draining and tiring. I told my mother I would fly home once my sister's body had made it home. The wait seemed to take forever. The local funeral home arranged the delivery of my sister's body at the Florida-Georgia line. The funeral director didn't ask how the expenses were going to be settled.

Once my sister's body was en route, I made my flight arrangements. I arrived home and continued to make arrangements. Since my sister wanted to be cremated, we didn't have to purchase a casket. We had to pay for the cremation, and we rented a casket for the memorial service and put some artificial flowers on top of the casket. My mother told me that people had been donating money and she had given it to the funeral director. However, there was still a very large outstanding balance.

We prepared ourselves for the wake to view her body. I honestly didn't think my mother was going to make it through this entire process all over again so soon. I felt like I was going to go insane from trying to be strong for everybody and hold this family together. I became angry with my father again. He had lost two children within a few weeks, and he was not there to be supportive of his family. I went from having three siblings to having just one.

Somehow, we made it through the wake. The next morning we prepared for the funeral. I pulled the funeral director aside and told him I would take care of the balance for my sister's funeral, and I thanked him for assisting our family. I also told him not to tell my mother, and if she were to ask about the payment, he was to tell her somebody had taken care of it for her.

The funeral service was wonderful. My youngest sister spoke as well as others from the community. I could not seem to get the strength to speak. I sat there thinking about my sister's laugh and her crazy personality. I was relieved in the knowledge that she didn't have to suffer before she passed.

At the end of the service, we made our way out the church. As I watched the pall barriers slide the casket into the hearse, I broke down and wept uncontrollably. There would be no going to the cemetery. This was it. My cousin, who is the pastor of the church, came to console me followed by other family members. I hadn't seen them in years. This seemed to make me more emotional.

We all gathered at my mother's house. She didn't want another repast. As I looked at all my nieces and nephews, I just smiled. I felt sad that the only time we came together as a family was for funerals. I remained at home for two more days. Each morning I would wake up at sunrise and head to the beach—my place of peace. I thanked God for another day as I sat with the sun beaming down on my face.

Once again, it was time to depart and head back to South Africa. This time I was returning with a colleague from the DC area who was coming back to assist with our office inspections. We arrived in South Africa where Jack was waiting for us. We took my colleague to her hotel and I went straight to bed. I didn't have any time to think about my siblings or to grieve. I shut down and got to the business of preparing for the office inspection. In some ways, this was great because I needed to keep my mind occupied. Working twelve-hour days didn't leave much time for me to think. I often found myself crying in the shower. The tears that I kept inside each day seemed to come out at night in those quiet moments when I was alone.

I was glad when my colleague prepared to leave. I felt like I just needed some time for me. Shortly after her departure, my childhood friend and her sister were coming over for a visit. It seemed as though I was non-stop busy, and I was neglecting my needs in the process. My supervisor at the time gave me a great gift. She treated me to an all-day pampering session at the spa in addition to giving me the day off. My body was so tense, and this treatment was just what I needed.

One of the hardest parts of having lost two siblings was accepting help, tokens of appreciation, and an assortment of gifts from others. I have always been the giver, and in my moments of weakness, I have had to learn to be a receiver. I had to learn to open my heart and my arms to allow others to pour themselves into my life. The hardest part was having the last words I'd spoken about my sister echoing in my mind. *She better have some damn life insurance when she dies.* I had told the funeral director I would send the check when I returned home. I had been home for over a month and I still hadn't sent the check. I finally told my mother to please let them know I was going to send the check, but for some reason, I couldn't bring myself to write the check.

It seemed as though writing the check would be my last and final say regarding my sister. I held on to her memory by not writing the check. Once I was able to write the check, I started to feel better, and I felt like I was released from the guilt I had been harboring.

Moving Forward

It was now mid-November, and I was busy preparing for the arrival of my friend and her sister, and planning for our big Thanksgiving dinner. Her visit was a welcomed one. I felt like I was starting to get back to myself. I had planned to go to work the following day after their arrival, but my supervisor told me to take the day off to enjoy my friends on their first night in our home. That night we drank three bottles of wine. We laughed and reminisced about our childhood days. I introduced them to South Africa and planned daily events for them to enjoy during my working hours. I arranged for a driver to come pick them up and take them on daily outings. They were in awe of this beautiful country. The weekend was filled with outings and shopping trips. They had a wonderful time during Thanksgiving as they met many of our friends and coworkers. We laughed, ate, and danced all night long. The last person didn't leave until one in the morning. We were exhausted as we sat on the edge of the pool, soaking our feet and drinking wine. What a great way to end the evening. A few days later, I bid farewell to my friends, the first ones to come visit us in South Africa.

After their departure, it was back to working long hours. My body felt like it was going to shut down from lack of rest. Soon it was January 2010, and we were running out of time to prepare for the inspection. I worked with an awesome team and we pulled it off. The night before the inspector's arrival, my supervisor and I prayed before closing up and going home. We had done all that we could do.

The inspection team arrived and gave us an outstanding rating. Those seemed like the longest four days of my life. It was finally over!

We arranged for the driver to come pick them up from the office and take them to the airport. Once they departed, my supervisor and I gave each other a high five and a hug. She and I went out for drinks to celebrate our hard work and accomplishments. The weight was lifted and we both went home and slept.

Life seemed to be getting back to normal until I found myself in a nightmare. I had a gut feeling regarding my husband and his possible infidelity. I started searching through his things not knowing what I was searching for. I went into his computer room and found a hard drive and a thumb drive filled with explicit photos. When he arrived home from his trip, I confronted him and he admitted to having an affair. I was so enraged that I broke every glass in the kitchen. As I cried and shouted at him, he told me that now I knew how he had felt when I'd had a fling on my cruise ship vacation. There were so many emotions running through my body. I didn't think we could get past this. When I asked Jack if he wanted to leave, he said no, and that he loved me and was not looking to leave. He told me I had no idea how I had hurt him in the past.

Despite all this, the trust in our relationship was gone. Once the initial anger and betrayal had diminished, and after many hours of talking, our relationship began to grow again. We rededicated ourselves to each other and agreed to be open and honest with each other in order to move forward in our marriage. Time was moving so fast, and I was so busy with work that I could not spend a lifetime having a pity party. It was now time to focus on the FIFA World Cup that South Africa was hosting. Once again, it seemed like I had no time to catch my breath.

There was going to be an influx of protectees in our district. I continued to pray and ask God to give us the strength we needed to handle this overwhelming task. I've learned that with God, nothing is impossible. We too made it through this major event and came shining through. Now I could focus on going home on home leave.

We were restricted from traveling during the World Cup. We departed the day before the final game in order to return in time for Quinton to start school. It was a good thing to be returning home without having to attend a funeral. However, my mother hadn't spread my sister's ashes in the Atlantic Ocean as she had requested. We planned to do this on my sister's birthday in July while I was there.

We arrived in Florida and it felt good to be home. When I arrived to my mother's house, I asked her where she kept my sister's ashes. She pointed to a corner of the room where a gift bag was sitting on the floor. I picked up the bag and opened the cardboard box. There she was in a thick plastic bag. This woman, who had been about 240 pounds, was reduced to a bag of ashes. Jack, my mother, Quinton, and I loaded up in the car and went to the inlet where we were to meet my nieces and nephews to release Wanda's ashes.

We waited and waited and none of them showed up. The kids had gotten into an argument and everything was put on hold. We put my sister's ashes back in the car and headed home. I wanted to stop on the bridge and drop her ashes into the water below. Once again this dysfunctional family had failed to come together to get something done.

Our trip back to the States was coming to an end, and it was time to return to South Africa. I was ready to come home. It was an exhausting trip, and I just wanted to get back and sleep in my own bed. Quinton and I returned so he could have a few days to rest before starting school. Jack stayed behind a few weeks longer to spend time with his sister who was recovering chemo treatments.

It was good to be back home. My housekeeper came and greeted us when we arrived. She asked to talk with me. She wanted to know if her pregnant daughter could stay in her quarters with her as she was going to deliver soon. I told her it was fine. I worried about this young lady because she seemed to be getting thinner and thinner.

I returned to work and was as busy as ever. Before I know it, the time had come for my childhood friend and her daughter's arrival. I was excited about them coming to visit. My friend had won a contest I had created called "Who knows Terran?" The contest was fun and exciting for all the ladies who participated. The winner won a round-trip ticket to South Africa. She paid for her daughter's ticket and they finally made it. I took them to different sites of interest, including Robben Island off the coast of Cape Town. She felt brave enough to rent a car while here and got around very well.

As we sat talking one night, I told her that I thought that her winning the trip was not about her but her daughter. I thought I was blessing my friend with this trip, but the purpose of the trip seemed to be so much more about the daughter than about her mother, my friend.

One evening my housekeeper came and told me that her daughter had delivered a baby girl. I congratulated her and told her she could go see her daughter the next day. Two days later, the daughter and baby came home. The housekeeper asked if she could stay in her room to help her with the baby. This beautiful little five-pound baby girl arrived. The housekeeper was taking care of her. Her daughter did nothing but sleep.

One Sunday afternoon about two and a half months later, the housekeeper came to our house clearly upset and crying. She asked if I could take her daughter to the hospital. She said her daughter was having trouble breathing. I ran to her room and saw that her daughter could barely talk, and she seemed to be gasping for air. Her body was even thinner and frailer than ever. I took the housekeeper outside and looked her in the eyes and said, "Don't lie to me; does your daughter have AIDS?"

"Yes ma'am, she does."

My God, this nineteen-year-old girl was on her deathbed and had just vaginally delivered this beautiful baby girl three months earlier. I took the housekeeper, her husband, her daughter, and the baby to the hospital. I returned home to tell my husband what had transpired.

On Monday morning, the housekeeper came into work and said she had spoken to her daughter, who sounded better and was regaining her strength. She told me she was going to the hospital to see her daughter on Tuesday after she finished working. That evening I told my housekeeper that she and I had to have a long talk about her daughter's situation. I explained that her daughter couldn't stay at the house once she was released from the hospital. I asked her if she was aware how sick her daughter was. It broke my heart to tell her why her daughter couldn't return to the house. "Namsa, your daughter is very sick. If she is released, she doesn't have much time to live based on her physical condition. I can't have her here because she could die on this property. I would be in a lot of trouble with the embassy, and I would have to answer a lot of questions regarding her death." She understood my position on this matter.

On Tuesday morning, my housekeeper called me at work sobbing. She informed me that the hospital called to tell her that her daughter had died. My heart felt as though it was going to fall out of my chest. I immediately came home to console her and found the other domestics from the neighborhood with her.

"My God, I'm so sorry," I whispered in her ear as I held her. She told me the hospital wanted her to claim the body and to let them know what funeral home would pick up the body. The hospital called two times while I was sitting there with her. She got herself together and we went to the public hospital. The hospital looked like a mental institution from the 1970s. I breathed a silent prayer of gratitude for being so blessed. *My God, thank you for insurance.*

We had to go up to the third floor of the hospital. The elevator looked as though it had not been inspected in years. It shimmied all the way up to the third floor, and when the doors creaked open slowly, I thought I was in the middle of a bad dream. We stepped out of the elevator and directly into a white painted cage, which was built to prevent anyone from leaving or entering. I wasn't sure if this was because this was the AIDS ward or not. We pressed a buzzer and a nurse came to the gate to let us in. We stood in the hall as the nurse went to get another nurse. I didn't understand anything they were saying. I looked down at the baby in my housekeeper's arms and thought *this is no place a baby should be*. Nothing looked clean. I felt like I would need to disinfect myself once I left.

The nurses led us to the room where the daughter's body lay. When they opened the door, the first thing I saw was the skeletal outline of her body under a sheet. The bed and all of the equipment looked decades old. The nurses departed the room and left us alone.

My housekeeper pulled back the sheet and gazed at her daughter. She let out a wail that only a mother could. I stood in the background and allowed the family to look at her. I eventually walked up to the side of the bed. I was horrified. I had never been in the same room with a dead person except at a funeral. She had lost even more weight since

Sunday, the day I had dropped her off at the hospital. There was only skin and bones. Her face was sunken in. I'm not sure why, but she had on a disposable diaper. I guess at some point she had lost control of her bowels, or she was simply too frail to go to the bathroom on her own.

We spent about twenty minutes in the room before my housekeeper said she was ready to leave. I didn't know what to say to console her.

When we returned home, she began preparing for the funeral. Family members arrived from other countries and friends rallied around her. She needed to go to her home in Mamelodi to finish the funeral arrangements. We packed the Jeep and I took her to her home. I had not yet seen the home that I had lent money for her husband to build. Not only was this place in a rough township area, it was up a mountain with no paved roads. It was a good thing I had a four-wheel drive Jeep to make it up this hill.

When we arrived, everybody began unloading her items. As soon I walked through the front door of her tiny house, I found myself in her bedroom. The house had two bedrooms that were separated by a bamboo partition. The kitchen was separated from the bedrooms by a wall, but I had to go outside to get to the kitchen. Although there were two small windows, it was dark inside the house. As I stood there just taking in every square foot, her husband and some men from the community disassembled her bed and put the mattress on the floor. The ladies swept the floor and cleaned the room. My housekeeper then sat on the mattress, and another lady came over and covered her with a huge thick blanket. As soon as it was draped around her shoulders, she let out a loud cry. All the ladies rallied with her on the floor, speaking a language I didn't understand. I felt out of place and at a loss. I didn't know what to do. I eventually sat on the mattress with the other ladies and put my arms around her, telling her it was going to be okay. She was sweating, as it was mid-November (summertime in the Southern Hemisphere), and she had this thick blanket wrapped around her. I asked if she wanted me to take it off her. She told me no; it was tradition.

As we sat there waiting for her youngest daughter to come home, I had an urge to use the bathroom. I didn't remember seeing a bathroom. I whispered in the housekeeper's ear and asked her where the bathroom was. A young lady took me outside and showed me a communal stall and handed me a roll of toilet paper. As I told her that was okay—I would just wait to go at home. I was thinking *you must be kidding.* It seemed like the urine I had in my bladder just dried up instantly. I thought about how many times I use the bathroom during the night and what I would do if I had to use this communal stall. "Thank you, Lord," was all I could say. I am humbled by each experience in South Africa.

Her daughter and her husband's youngest sister arrived home from school. I again heard them speaking a language I didn't understand. I saw this young girl pass out in her mother's lap. Almost everybody in the room started crying and what I think was praying. It sounded like a Pentecostal church full of women speaking in tongues. I was moved and shaken by the sorrow that filled the room. I picked up her daughter and led her outside to get some air. As I held her, I told her that they were going to be okay. I asked her to please be strong for her mother. She nodded in agreement. I gave her a glass of water that a lady handed me. The same lady offered me a glass of water, but I politely declined by shaking my head no.

More neighbors started to arrive as news spread throughout the township. It was starting to get dark and I knew I couldn't stay much longer. I was alone in a high crime area that was not familiar to me. I went back inside and told my housekeeper that I had to go home, as it was getting dark. She hugged me and held me so tight as if she didn't want me to leave, but I knew she was in good hands with the grannies and other ladies from the community.

When I got in my car, I programed my GPS to take me home. I didn't remember how to get down from the mountain, as it did not register on the GPS. I locked the doors and prayed that I would make it home safely. As I drove through the town, I had to stop at only one traffic light, and I prayed I wouldn't get stuck at the red light. I felt like a sitting target in this big Jeep with diplomatic tags. It was not the norm to see such a vehicle in this area, not to mention the tags.

I made it home safely. I was dusty and dirty from the unpaved roads and the wind moving the dirt around and about. When my husband arrived home, I told him about my experience. I showered and prayed for this family as I prepared to go to bed. When I arrived at work the next day, I told my supervisor of the event from the day before. "Girl, you can't make up this kind of stuff," she said in dismay. I told her the funeral was going to be Saturday, and I was going to attend out of respect but out of curiosity also. My housekeeper had told me that the funeral home would bring her daughter's body home on Friday and the body would remain in the house overnight for burial the next day. My mouth fell open when she told me this. I asked her if she would sleep in the house with a dead body and she said yes; it's tradition. *Good Lord, I think I have heard it all.*

On Friday, Jack and I returned to the mountain. There was a tent set up outside and people were sitting around singing and praying. I went inside the house and saw my housekeeper sitting in the same spot on the mattress wrapped in the blanket. I went to greet her and hug her. We talked briefly before I returned outside with Jack.

Shortly after stepping outside, I was called back inside. My housekeeper told me the funeral home people were at the base of the mountain and the hearse could not make it up the mountain. She asked if my husband had rope in the car, and if so, could he pull them up. Once again, when I think I have seen and heard it all, something outdoes the last incident. Jack went down the mountain, and after some time, he returned with the hearse in tow. They used rope and a water hose to pull it up the hill. The funeral directors greeted my housekeeper and set up a partition in her room. I went outside as they prepared to bring the body inside. "My God," I whispered to myself when I saw the casket. It was nothing like the caskets we're used to in the United States. It was a narrow wooden coffin shaped like a V. It looked like something you'd see in a vampire movie.

The funeral director set the coffin on a stand behind the partition and left. He then returned with two wreaths of flowers that my supervisor and I had purchased. The ladies of the village began to sing and rally around my housekeeper and her daughter. I asked her if they were going to open the coffin, and she told me that I could view her daughter's body if I wanted to. I told her I would wait until the next day during the funeral. I looked at the innocent baby I was holding who would never know her mother. She was such a beautiful little girl.

This very special little girl's mother had died from AIDS and she was born negative. I whispered in her ear that God was going to take care of her because she is very special.

We returned the next day for the funeral. I had asked my housekeeper if there was something specific I should wear, as I didn't want to offend anyone. I wore a simple sleeveless black dress and hat. Jack and Quinton wore suits. When we arrived at my housekeeper's house, we felt overdressed. I went into the house to greet my housekeeper and her daughter. The house was filled with the neighborhood ladies. I also met her pastor. There were people sitting under the tent, people I didn't know and had never met. One of the ladies was holding the baby, and she was crying and fussing. I took her and started talking to her, and she recognized my voice and settled down. Before the pastor opened the coffin, my housekeeper asked me to cover my head and shoulders before viewing the body. All the ladies lined up and walked up to the coffin. There she lay in a box, body frail and very small.

I noticed that none of the men came into the house. I asked my housekeeper could men come in and she said no, but she would allow Jack and Quinton to come in to see the body. They chose not to come into the house. The funeral home personnel had arrived. However, they were stuck down the hill again. Jack and Quinton went down the hill to pull them up.

They came inside the house and closed the coffin. My housekeeper and all the ladies cried, screamed, and wept. They moved the coffin under the tent and conducted the funeral right there in front of the house. My housekeeper and her family sat on the ground near the coffin. People came forward and spoke, again in a language I didn't understand. My housekeeper had asked me to say some words. I looked at the program and saw my name on the program. The pastor asked me to come forward. I stood in front of a bunch of strangers with the baby in my arms, speaking very slowly so they could understand what I was saying.

The service had concluded and it was time to go to the cemetery. They loaded the body in the hearse and we gave our housekeeper and others a ride down the hill as the family car could not make it up the hill. The people of the village walked downhill behind the hearse, singing. It was a very moving scene. Later I wished I had recorded the entire process.

At the bottom of the hill, a large city bus was waiting. Everybody boarded the bus to be taken to the cemetery. We followed the procession to the cemetery. There was a covered area with chairs, similar to what one would see at an American gravesite. The pastor started the service and then the housekeeper gave him a bag of items to be placed in the grave. These included some of her daughter's clothes and a teddy bear. She also gave him a blanket to drape over the coffin. The coffin was manually lowered into the grave, at which time a funeral attendant came and collected the programs from everybody. They then put them in the grave. A row of men from the village stood on either side of the gravesite. They manually took turns with shovels covering the coffin. When this was completed, it looked like a big anthill of dirt. They then placed rocks around the mound to keep the dirt from shifting. We all returned to our perspective vehicles to return to the housekeeper's home for the repast. As people returned to the house, a church member splashed water on them; then they would turn around and he would do the same to their back. I was standing there holding the baby, telling the housekeeper that we would be going home soon, and before I knew it was coming, I was doused with water. I was now standing there soaking wet with the baby in my arms. I almost started cussing before I was doused again. I asked the housekeeper why this man was wetting everybody. She told me it was a symbolic cleansing after leaving the gravesite before eating. I wished he had warned me.

I told her I had a couple of questions about the burial process. I asked why she wasn't covered in the blanket, and she said she could come from under the blanket after the burial. I told her I forgot that I had my program in my purse and I didn't turn it in to be placed in the grave. I asked if I would be cursed as a result. She laughed and said no, and that it was okay that I kept it.

This entire funeral process was so different from what I was used to, but so beautiful at the same time. Tradition is so important to Africans. I don't fully agree with or understand the reasons behind some of the things they do, but I have much respect for their tenacity in holding on to their traditions.

I asked my housekeeper how much time she needed off work, and she told me two weeks. I told her that was fine. When I returned home, I looked at the calendar and saw that Thanksgiving would fall in those two weeks. She had been my help during the holiday in previous years. I started to think of who I could get to help me with the preparations of feeding more than forty people. I knew I would not only need her but another helper this year. I asked the young lady who cleaned our office. She was elated that I would ask her to help me. After a week passed, I called the housekeeper to check on her and asked her if she could recommend another lady to assist me during the holiday.

She said, "Ma'am, I will come back. Another lady don't know what needs to be done, and you have too many jewelry all over the place." I asked if she was sure, and she insisted on coming back. I loved her dedication and commitment to me.

I went to pick up her and the baby. They came home the day before Thanksgiving. We were in the kitchen doing our usual tasks to get ready for the next day. Thanksgiving came and we had our usual house full of old and new friends. Everybody was in love with the baby and passed her around. She was such a good baby. Another year and Thanksgiving was such a success. I was tired and every part of my body ached. I had missed my housekeeper. It seemed like she had been gone forever.

While she was gone, I was thinking about how HIV/AIDS was killing so many people in this country. I thought about how my housekeeper was now taking care of a baby because her young daughter had died from AIDS. I've known people with HIV/AIDS, but her loss was so personal to me. During the month of December, which is HIV/AIDS awareness month, USAID sponsors free HIV testing. I told my housekeeper that I wanted to take her, her other daughter, and anybody else she knew to be tested because they could live longer if they got treatment if they tested positive for HIV/AIDS. I also told her that to reduce the stigma, I would be tested also.

I loaded up a car full of ladies and took them to be tested. After the testing, I exchanged my test results with each one of the ladies. They didn't exchange their results with each other, but they trusted me and allowed me to see theirs. Some were positive. I talked to them as a group about the importance of knowing their CD count and getting medication. I was amazed at how eager they were to be informed. One lady started going to the clinic on a regular basis, and she even brought her lab work for me to see that her CD count was going up. Another young lady wanted to know when free testing would be held again. One lady had insisted that her husband get tested. I was shocked at how much they yearned for more information. I wasn't a doctor, but they trusted me enough to share their information and ask questions. This was a huge milestone because so many people don't even want to talk about HIV/AIDS because of the stigma. I could only hope they would remain this vigilant.

Now that the funeral and holidays were behind us, I told Jack that I was so ready for a break. It was time for us to plan our vacation. I've always wanted to go to Cairo, see the pyramids, and ride a camel. Just as we started to plan our trip, however, Cairo erupted in civil war in what is now known as the Arab Spring. The streets were on fire and there was chaos all over. The Department of State issued a travel warning to Cairo, Egypt. I couldn't believe what I was seeing on the news. I had to start thinking very fast of an alternative place to go.

I started searching and somehow came up with Dubai, UAE. We had never been to the Middle East. I started my research to plan our activities and things to do and see. I contacted my travel agent and asked her to find us a nice hotel. The government would provide our air transportation. She booked us into the Grand Hyatt Dubai. Everything was set and we were excited. In my research, I read that since this is a Muslim country, there must be no public displays of affection. They also advised on wearing proper attire, even though Dubai isn't as strict as some of the neighboring countries are in regards to clothing.

We arrived in Dubai after an eight-hour flight. Clearing through customs was a breeze, unlike the horror stories I had read about people being detained for various reasons. Our driver was waiting for us as we exited the airport. I was in awe of the architectural skyline. All the buildings seemed so tall. When we arrived at the hotel, the entrance seemed magical. There was gold inlay surrounding the marble tile, and the marble columns extended high into the ceiling. After checking in, we took a walk around the grounds. This hotel had everything a person could ever want without leaving the grounds. The inside gardens were so beautiful that you'd almost forget you were in a building. There were several restaurants, with each offering a variety of delicious foods.

Our first excursion was sand dune bashing in 4 x 4 trucks. What a thrill ride. Nothing but sand and desert as far as the eyes can see. We took a break on top of a high sand dune and I sat and looked around me. There was nothing but mountains of sand. As I sat there gazing over the horizon, I thought how blessed I am to be in such a beautiful location. I had to pinch myself as I thought about the little black girl from the government housing projects who was now on vacation in the Middle East. There was nothing out there but open space, but it was one of the most beautiful and amazing places that I had ever been.

Our day trip ended with dinner back at the base camp. The food was very interesting and different. With our adventurous spirit, we tried a little of everything. The entertainment was nice also. It was here that I got my first henna drawing on the back of my hand. The highlight of the evening was to fulfill one of many dreams I've had for a long time. I wanted to ride a camel. After dinner, we got on quad bikes and rode around the desert. Somehow, Jack managed to get stuck and I had to go back to the base camp to get help. After that little adventure, we decided to ride the camels. I couldn't believe I was actually going to ride a camel. We climbed on, and as the camel got up from its sitting position, it felt like it had hydraulics on its legs. I was so excited. I felt like a kid at an amusement park. What a way to end the day.

As we were packing up getting ready to leave the campsite, I looked up at the top of one of the tallest sand dunes and saw what I thought was a beautiful sight. The moon was full, and at the top of the sand dune ridge, the camel handler was walking with a caravan of camels silhouetted against the evening sky. It looked like a scene out of a movie, and the moon appeared to be their guiding light.

The next few days we spent time touring and sightseeing Dubai. Everything seemed so big. We took pictures of the World's only seven-star hotel on the beach. We went to the Gold Souk market where there

was so much gold down row after row of allies and streets. We had a
chance to see the world's biggest ring, all made of 22-24 karat gold.
My gift to myself was an ankle bracelet and a ring. The malls were
massive in size. We went to Ski Dubai, a ski slope inside a mall. We also
went to an aquarium located in a mall and rode the glass-bottom boat.

As we met many local workers, we learned that nobody seemed
to be from Dubai. The majority of the workers in Dubai are foreign-
ers. Many Dubaians do not work, as their income is subsidized by the
government's oil profits. The country is very wealthy and developing
at a very fast pace.

Our trip to Dubai was one of the best vacations we had taken.
It was educational, interesting, and relaxing. As our plane took off,
we looked down to catch a bird's-eye view of the Palm—a manmade
island in the shape of a palm tree that sits in the ocean. What a spectacular view.

Now that the vacation was over it was time to return to work and
prepare for the arrival of my new supervisor. I anxiously awaited his
arrival since we had been without a supervisor for four months. We
had three new personnel, and I was the only one with all the institu-
tional knowledge trying to get everybody settled into their new jobs.
After he arrived, we invited him to Easter Sunday church service
and dinner. There was a lot to do regarding getting him settled and
acclimated to his new assignment. He fell right in and everything was
working just fine. The workload started to increase and it seemed like
I was in need of another break. People often say that we take a lot of
vacations. My reply to them is that I work hard; therefore, I play hard.
I tried to plan a wedding anniversary get-a-way for Jack and me, but
Quinton would be on school break during that time, so I decided to
make it a family trip.

I had heard nice things about Zanzibar, Tanzania. I found a wonderful all-inclusive package that even included round-trip airfare. I
contacted my travel agent, and everything was set; soon, we were off
to Tanzania. When we landed, my first thought was *this looks nothing like
the resort*. The airport only had one airstrip. When we disembarked, our
luggage was sitting in the middle of the floor of the airport. There was
no luggage conveyor going around and around. It was extremely hot

and my hair immediately went poofy. As we made our way through customs and to the outside, there were a lot of men trying to offer us a ride.

Through the crowd, I could see our driver holding a sign with our name on it. He greeted us and escorted us to our transportation. On arriving, we were given bottles of water and cool wet towels to wash our hands and face. As we made the hour drive to the resort, I kept hoping to see the beautiful place I had seen online. As we rode through the towns, I noticed how all the houses seemed to be incomplete. The raw brick blocks were exposed with no finishing to them. It appeared that the people were concerned about shelter and not the external façade of the houses.

Finally, we arrived at the resort. After what we had seen on the long drive, it felt like we had stepped into a different world. The grounds and landscape were immaculate. We were greeted at the reception area with a glass of cold juice and escorted to the reception desk. As we were escorted to our rooms, I felt like I was in paradise. Our rooms faced the Indian Ocean, and they were decorated in a cozy, chic décor. We could sit on the balcony and watch the tides coming in and out. We could wake up in the morning to the ocean breeze. This was paradise.

We woke up the next day ready for our first excursion, which was snorkeling. We were driven to the pickup area where we boarded some very old-looking wooden boats. The tides were so low that we walked into the ocean to go aboard. We started to sail out and the shoreline disappeared. The crew cut the tops off coconuts and we drank the fresh juice. As we continued to sail, we saw a school of dolphins alongside the boat. This was our first time seeing dolphins in the wild. The boat came to a stop. Our guide told us this was where we would snorkel. I was a bit fearful, as this was only my second time snorkeling, and we were not given life vests as had been done the first time. This time we were only given flippers. I got into the water with my heart beating so fast. I just knew I would not stay afloat. Despite my fears, however, I floated on my belly and realized I wasn't sinking. The fish and coral below were spectacular. We took many pictures with our underwater camera. We boarded the boat, and then we were taken to another area where the underwater scene was even more beautiful.

We boarded the boat again, as it was time to have lunch on a distant island. As we came near the shore, the boat stopped in the ocean and we disembarked in the same manner that we had embarked: stepping into the water and walking to the shore. The tides were so low that it was safe and easy to do. We arrived at our location, unpacked our gear, and went for a swim in the ocean while lunch was being prepared. The Indian Ocean is so warm. We were called in for lunch and they started with a variety of exotic fruits I had never seen before. We were all up for the challenge to try a little bit of everything. Some items were very good, while others looked very pretty but lacked any taste. It was now time for the main course. There were several types of seafood, and lots of side dishes that we were not familiar with at all, but everything was very good. After lunch, I walked along the beach and bought fabric and scarfs from a local vendor. I didn't have to haggle much with the vendor as she gave me a really good discount.

As the day went on, I noticed the tides had started to come in. By the end of lunch, the area we had walked on was now underwater. I wondered how we were going to get back to the boats. Not to worry—this was the norm for them, and they just moved the boats to another area where the water was shallower. We boarded the boats and headed back, but we made one last stop to an area of mangroves. The water was shallow and very warm. It was also much saltier than in the ocean. We learned that the mangroves make the water in that area much more salty. As we headed back to our original location, the sun was setting. It was a beautiful sight.

We arrived back at the resort and cleaned ourselves up for dinner. There was so much food on the buffet bar. Again, we tried things we had never seen or heard of before. The following day we took a tour around Zanzibar and a boat ride to Prison Island. This excursion was very informative and a great learning experience. We learned about the slave trade from East Africa. We visited a site where slaves were held in a very small and dark area that is now underneath a church. There is so much history in this area. It was sad and such a surreal experience. We were then taken to Prison Island where we saw the biggest turtle I had ever seen. The island was rather rundown. The guide took us to an area that would have been the door of no return. Once a slave stepped through the door, it lead to a dock where the slave would have boarded a ship and been sent to one of the Caribbean islands. Standing there, it was almost like hearing the cries from the past.

When we arrived back at the resort, we changed into our swim-wear and went for a walk on the beach. People were selling all sorts of things. They were in awe to see black Americans. A group of ladies sat with me and I agreed to let them do a henna drawing. This lady started at my finger and went up my arm to my elbow. The design came out beautifully. I fell in love with henna drawings all over again. After getting my henna done, we continued to walk down the beach where there were a bunch of men from the Massai tribe. We struck up a very interesting conversation with them as they lured us into their shops to buy their goods. They did not believe we were Americans. They told us only white people live in America. We told them the story of how blacks came to live in America because of the slave trade from West Africa. They were in such shock to learn this.

We asked them to jump in the air for us like we had seen on TV. They could jump amazingly high. They shared their stories of how they ended up in Zanzibar from Kenya. Many had left their families to come to Zanzibar for a better life. These young men told us stories of how they wanted to attend school but could not because they had to provide for their families. We took many pictures with them. They were very fond of Quinton, and they didn't believe his age because they said he was too tall to be sixteen years old. We bought some of their goods and said our goodbyes.

As we were walking back to the resort, my heart felt so heavy. I was enjoying a vacation and these young men only wanted an education. I find it so disheartening to be on a continent that is so wealthy with all its natural minerals yet there is still such poverty. A basic education is out of reach for so many. We Americans take so much for granted. I am so humbled every time I encounter people like these young men. What a way to end this trip.

The vacation was much in order and really needed, but it was time to return to the real world of working long hours. It was also time to start planning our annual Thanksgiving Day dinner/party. Each year we say that we are going to cut the number of people we're inviting, but the number keeps increasing. The more people we meet, the more we want them to share in our holiday. To make things even more complicated this year, many of the families we invited had children. By the time the RSVP was completed, we had a total of fifty people planning to come, including children. Good grief, what was I thinking? I ordered a jumping castle for the kids to entertain themselves. This was our fourth Thanksgiving dinner and the housekeeper knew what had to be done. I think she got a rush in preparing for this day every year. I also hired an additional lady to assist us with the preparations.

It's a lot of work, but there is a good feeling in hosting this event every year. Our friends are a very diverse group of people, and it's nice to see everybody mingle, getting to know one another. I also love to capture these moments on film and look back at how these people would not have ordinarily come together like this. There is still a problem with race relations in this country, but when they are here at our house, we laugh together, eat together, dance together, and have a ball. Even if it's just for one day, I feel blessed to bring this diverse crowd together.

One of the traditions we established during the Thanksgiving dinner is that we gather in a circle before we pray, and we all introduce ourselves and say where we're from. We have had people from all over Africa at these dinners, people from different walks of life and from different socio-economic backgrounds. Here, nobody is better than the next person. Attitudes are checked and left at the front gate.

I always take the next day off to arrange for the tables, chairs, silverware, table linens, and other items that need to be picked up. It is great that the embassy provides all these things for us to use.

Before I knew it, it was Christmas time. It's still hard getting in the Christmas spirit when it's 90 degrees outside. As tradition would have it, Jack is traveling and Quinton and I pull out the tree to decorate it only days before Christmas. I'm not sure why we go through the motion of putting it up because it doesn't stay up that long. It's not like we have small children in the house anymore. I guess once Quinton leaves home Jack and I won't even bother with putting one up. Maybe we'll be in some tropical place and a Christmas tree won't even be on our radar. I do find it funny that regardless of how old Quinton is, he still gets up early in the morning on Christmas Day like a little kid. We manage to drag ourselves out of bed shortly after him. Christmas is our family time. We laugh as we eat breakfast and exchange gifts. It is our quiet time to be away from our extended family and friends. We are reminded of how blessed we are as a family.

The Long Journey Home

It was January 1, 2012, and we were ringing in the New Year! I find it funny how it is the New Year here when it's only 6:00 p.m. in the United States. We claimed that 2012 was going to be our year and great things would unfold for us. I felt like God was going to shine on us. We welcome each new year with great expectation, but I was more excited about this year. I felt it was going to be a refreshing beginning.

Jack was still traveling a lot in his job, and the opportunity arose for me to accompany him on a trip to Botswana. I was excited because I had not been to Botswana yet, and it is a short one-hour plane ride from South Africa. I arranged for my supervisor and his wife to look after Quinton during this three-day weekend. I flew into this dry, dusty country with no expectations except to enjoy the change and spend some quality time with Jack. There was not a lot to do, as he had to work one day. One of his colleagues invited us over for dinner, and we sat around socializing and having a good time. Before I knew it, it was time to return home.

Shortly after I returned Jack also returned home. He had been complaining of pain in his upper abdomen lately, and the pain had intensified. We both thought it was a bad case of indigestion and dismissed it. The weekend came and he still wasn't feeling any relief. He woke up on Sunday morning with a fever and stayed in bed most of the day. I gave him fever reducers around the clock to no avail. I suggested he go the doctors at the embassy in the morning. He went to the doctor and they referred him to the emergency room. The doctors told him he had a urinary tract infection and took an X-ray of his chest. They referred him to an internal medicine doctor the next day.

The internal medicine doctor reviewed his X-ray and suggested Jack have an MRI done on his chest area as the X-ray showed an unidentifiable image. He also stated that Jack's blood work showed that there was more going on inside his body that needed to be addressed. Jack said the pain in his abdomen was affecting his breathing, causing discomfort. I was very worried about him. We kept the embassy doctor abreast of what was transpiring.

On March 16, 2012, I accompanied Jack to the internal medicine doctor for the results of all the tests and the MRI. The doctor came in with Jack's file in his hand. When he opened it up, his facial expression changed. He said, "Mr. Jackson, we are dealing with a serious problem. The MRI and blood work have confirmed that you have pancreatic cancer. I want to order another series of blood tests." My heart almost jumped out of my chest when the word cancer came out of his mouth. Jack just calmly said, "Okay, so what do we do next?" The doctor suggested that he should biopsy the mass that was showing on his pancreas. He also suggested that Jack should have the procedure done back in the United States, and have it done immediately. Jack told him he was scheduled to travel the next week, and he would schedule the procedure after returning home.

The doctor said, "No, Mr. Jackson, I suggest you do *not* travel until we have all the tests done."

Jack, responded with his usual easy-going manner, and just chuckled and said, "Okay," but when he looked at the doctor, who had a very stoic look on his face, Jack's expression changed to a more serious one. The doctor stated that he wished the news were better.

Jack and I got up and walked hand in hand back to our car. There were few words spoken as we took in the news. We were both in a state of shock and disbelief. I told Jack that regardless of what was going on in his body, we were going to fight this hand in hand.

When we got home, I called the embassy to make an appointment with the embassy doctor. They had received the results from all the tests. The nurse put me through directly to the doctor. He told me he was booked solid with appointments, and he wanted to wait until he had an open window to spend time to go over the results. He made the appointment for three days later.

When we entered the medical unit on the appointed day, the nurses hugged us and offered their support and prayers. We met with the doctor, and he told us that based on the results of the tests, it looked like there was a mass on the pancreas, and all signs pointed to pancreatic cancer. Jack asked him to be honest with him about how much time he had to live. The doctor said he had about six months. My heart felt like it was going to jump out of my chest. In six months, it would be September: Jack's birthday month. All I could do was murmur "my God...my God." The doctor was very patient in answering all our questions and giving us the outlook.

Jack told him that he had opted not to receive treatment. He stated that his quality of life was more important than quantity, and he didn't want to spend the rest of his time going through chemo when the outlook for this disease is very gloomy. I supported his decision because his mother and sister had died from cancer, and he knew first-hand how this was going to affect him and his quality of life. We asked the doctor if he could tell us what stage Jack's cancer was at based on the X-ray film and blood tests. He said around stage three.

At the end of our appointment, the doctor asked if he could pray with us. We gathered in the center of his office and held hands, and he began to pray. As he was praying, I was thanking God for this God-fearing doctor who obviously knew the power of prayer. After we prayed, the doctor told us that he could only do so much as a doctor, and in the end, God had the last word concerning Jack's life despite what the medical professionals might say.

Before we departed, he told us that he was working on getting Jack sent to the United States by med-evac for the biopsy. We told him we would rather go back to Atlanta because there were great hospitals there, and we would have a host of friends to support us while we are there.

We left the doctor's office shaken but not broken. We both went back to work. Around mid-day, I had an emotional breakdown. The thought of being a single mother to my son, and not having my best friend in my life anymore, made my heart ache. There were so many thoughts running through my mind. If we had to return to the United States, where were we going to stay? We had renters in our house in

Atlanta. A few tears turned into wailing. I felt like I couldn't breathe. I felt sick at the stomach.

One of my coworkers came to check on me, and I told him the news we had just been given. I managed to regain my composure and told him I needed air and I needed to put something in my stomach. He offered to get my lunch, but I told him I felt like I needed to get out of the office and walk. He told me that was fine, but he was going with me. I decided on a fast food place around the corner from the office. The air felt good. I felt like I could breathe again. We returned to the office and I managed to remain at work the entire day.

When I arrived home, Jack and I talked about our options, and how he wanted to proceed. He said he had to let the kids know. He called each one and broke the news to them. We tried to decide on how much information we should tell Quinton. We didn't want to tell him that Jack only had six months to live. We wanted him to stay focused on his schoolwork, and we didn't want him to worry about when was his dad was going to die.

We sat Quinton down and told him that his dad had cancer, and he was going to be treated for it. We told him that our lives were going to change because his dad might be weak and sick as he went through the treatment. We did not tell him that his dad only had six months to live. We also told him that as time went on, we would need him help out around the house more. I'm not sure how he processed the news; he said he was sad, but he didn't really display any emotion.

As Jack and I prepared for bed, we held hands and prayed. We prayed that God was going to work this all out in our favor. I told Jack that God couldn't take him away from us just yet. I prayed some years ago that God would allow Jack to live until Quinton was grown and out of the house. I told Jack that God wouldn't leave me to raise Quinton alone. As I laid there in the bed, I began to cry. I couldn't seem to stop myself. Jack held me and assured me that everything would be okay. I told him I just couldn't imagine life without his laughter. I couldn't imagine life without his touch. He pulled me closer and just held me. Until this point, Jack had not shown any real emotions. He had just kept saying, "God's will." Now he suddenly broke down and started to cry. I held him and told him everything was going to be okay.

I told him that I was glad to see him cry because I worried about all that he had kept bottled up inside, and it was okay to let it out. It was okay to be afraid of the unknown.

My supervisor was traveling, so I sent him an email saying that I would need him and his wife to assist with Quinton because the medical unit was going to med-evac Jack back to the United States for further testing. When he arrived back in the office, I gave him all the information that had been given to us. I started to cry again as I replayed the story in my mind. I told him that Jack was okay with all of this, and that his only response was to say, "If it's God's will, then it's okay."

I started to pack, not knowing when we were going to get the call to fly back to the States. As I was looking into flight prices, I got an email from my former supervisor. The email had originated from my current supervisor to our headquarters in Washington, DC. He had requested that I be placed on a temporary assignment to the Atlanta office. I was confused; surely, he didn't expect me to go to work while I was in Atlanta. I told him about the email, and he said it was supposed to be a private email. He was requesting that I be assigned to Atlanta so my job could pay for my ticket and I wouldn't have to pay for it. After he explained his plan, it made sense. I thanked him for being so considerate. My eyes began to tear up again as I thought of him being willing to do this for me. I was so overwhelmed with all the offers of support and sincere good wishes. I told my supervisor's wife that we had always been givers, and it was a learning process to be on the receiving end. I was so appreciative.

On Monday, March 26, at 7:30 p.m., we got a call stating that we had to be in Atlanta on Wednesday morning at 11:00 a.m. for Jack to have the biopsy. My heart started to race because that would mean we would have to leave the next day in order to arrive in Atlanta on Wednesday. We quickly moved into fourth gear. I phoned my supervisor and told him we had just gotten the phone call. I talked to his wife regarding the arrangements for Quinton. I called the housekeeper and told her. We went over to my supervisor's house so that she could meet them and know who was going to be in charge of Quinton while we were gone. My mind was running a hundred miles an hour. I went to work the next day to finish up some things in the office, and then I went to get a manicure and pedicure. As I lay there getting my feet done, the owner of the salon came and gave me a gift certificate for a free full body massage. I began to cry again. She said she thought I could use this, and that I could bring Jack for a free massage, too. She asked if I was okay. I told her I was fine and the tears were tears of joy and appreciation. I told her that there had been such an outpouring of support for us from so many of our South African friends.

I came home and emailed our friends back in Atlanta to alert them of our return. So many of them invited us to stay in their homes while we were in town. I told Jack that I was going to make reservations at a hotel as I didn't want to offend anybody, and it would be better for us to have time alone after the biopsy. I informed our friends of our lodging plans and they all understood.

Jack's doctor called to say that he didn't understand what was going on, as Jack's blood work was constantly changing and he couldn't explain the changes. I told Jack that God had already started to change this situation around for the good. As we sat on the bed, Jack told me he didn't want me to get my hopes up just to be let down. I told him I had no choice but to believe that this entire situation was going to be turned around. I told him I couldn't think otherwise. I said, "All I have right now is my faith. I can't let go of that; it is all I have to hold on to." I told him I was fighting for both of us.

I told my supervisor that I thanked him for trying to get me reassigned, but the government was going to pay my ticket to accompany Jack back to the States. We went over everything regarding Quinton, and then it was time for us to leave. I told Quinton we love him, and I would call to check on him as soon as I could.

The driver arrived to pick us up. The housekeeper saw us off, and I told her I would be in touch once we were settled. The ride to the airport seemed like the longest ride of my life. My heart felt so heavy and full. I wanted to cry, but I had done so much crying already, and I didn't want Jack to worry about me.

Finally, we boarded the plane. Unfortunately, we were seated next to a woman with an infant. This baby cried for at least twelve to fourteen hours of the sixteen-hour flight. He became sick and started throwing up all over the place. We didn't get any sleep, and she struggled to keep the baby quiet. She even asked me to hold him at one point as she was trying to get something from the overhead bin. *Dear God, please give us some relief,* I prayed.

We arrived safely in Atlanta. As we were departing, the airline attendants thanked us for being so patient. I just smiled and kept walking. We had a matter of hours to get our luggage, pick up the rental car, check into the hotel, and shower in order to make it to the hospital by 11:00 a.m.

We made it in time for his appointment. I was feeling very anxious as we waited in the pre-op room. They finally came and took Jack back. I kissed him and told him everything was going to be okay. As they wheeled him away, I pray, *Dear God, please watch over my husband. Please keep him under your care. Please be in the operating room and allow the doctor to perform this procedure without any problems. Dear God, please heal his body right now in the name of Jesus.*

It seemed like the procedure was taking forever. I went to the hospital cafeteria to get something to eat. I returned to the waiting area and sent out a few emails letting people know we had arrived safely. After what seemed to be hours, the doctor came out and called my name. He said the procedure went well and they would be bringing Jack down shortly. He said he suctioned out a lot of fluid around the pancreas. He said he wouldn't get the pathology report until after Monday. I told him we were departing on Monday and would like to take the report back with us. They brought Jack down and there were bloodstains on his gown. His voice was raspy and his throat was sore from the procedure. He said he felt he could breathe a little easier and didn't feel the pressure in his chest. I told him the doctor had removed a lot of fluid during the procedure.

Jack was released from the hospital and we went back to the hotel room to get some much-needed rest. Later that evening, we went out for dinner. We didn't talk much about the procedure. We returned to the hotel room and went to bed. I told Jack that it was my belief that God had worked in our favor.

The following day, we woke up early in the morning and drove to our old neighborhood to look at our house. Everything seemed to be in order from the outside. We ran into our next-door neighbor and told her why we were back. She, like so many others, said she would keep us in her prayers.

We then went to a restaurant where our friends had gathered to show their support for us. We knew we wouldn't have time to go around and visit people individually, so we met them all at a restaurant. It was so wonderful to see everybody. My childhood friend drove from Virginia with her daughter to be with us. I thought this was so special and thoughtful of her. The last couple to arrive was my former intern, who was like an adopted son to me, and his fiancé and their daughter. I started to cry all over again. I thought, *gosh, people really do love us*. We had a wonderful time fellowshipping with everybody. I think it was really good for Jack, and it lifted his spirits immeasurably. It was good to laugh and not think about cancer for a few hours.

After the lunch, I went back to the hotel room to wait for another friend who was traveling from Virginia with her mother. Jack went to an electronics store to buy some gadgets. It was so good to see my friend whom I had met when we were in the military. I was also her daughter's godmother, as I was there with her for the delivery. I hadn't seen her mother in over twenty years. It was such a wonderful reunion. After waiting for Jack to return, we decided to go over to the store and meet him over there. We stood in the parking lot and talked for hours. It was time for my friend and her mother to continue their journey to Macon, Georgia. Again, I was smiling with joy because my friend took the time to come see me.

Later in the evening, two more of our friends wanted to come by the room because they couldn't make it to the lunch. We sat around the pool area and had a wonderful time with them, but the jetlag started to kick in and we were so tired. Our friends departed and we went to bed. Like the previous morning, I was awake at 3:00 a.m. I wrote my supervisor to check in on Quinton and the office. They were taking good care of him. I went back to bed and we woke up at around 9:00 a.m. Jack and I would spend the day getting our driver's licenses renewed, and we planned to do some shopping to send back some boxes of goodies. We went out to our favorite restaurants and laughed about anything and everything. We continued to lift each other up at different times. It seemed like all we had was each other.

Later in the evening, the doctor who had performed the biopsy called to give us the result. Jack was resting, so I took the call. He said, "Mrs. Jackson, I'm calling because the pathology report has come back. Your husband does not have pancreatic cancer. However, he does have lymphoma—B-cell lymphoma." He went on to say that this was a form of cancer of the immune system. "This is the lesser of two evils," he added. My mind was racing, as I had no idea what lymphoma was and whether it was treatable.

Jack woke up while I was talking to the doctor and writing down all this information. I asked the doctor what stage the cancer was in. He told me that Jack's doctor would have to look at all the pathology reports and tell us that information. I asked him if we could pick up a copy of the report to take back with us. He told us it would be ready on Monday morning. "Thank you Jesus," I said under my breath. Then I said to the doctor, "We are leaving Monday evening, so we'll pick up the report in the morning. Thank you so much for everything."

After hanging up with the doctor, I filled Jack in on the parts of the conversation he hadn't heard. I immediately turned on my computer and started researching lymphoma. We read and read and read. It was still confusing regarding the prognosis, but knowing this was a little better than pancreatic cancer felt like a ton of bricks had been lifted off our shoulders. I cried tears of joy with some anxiety mixed in because we still didn't know the stage the cancer was in. I wanted to rush back home with these results to get a better picture of what we were dealing with.

On Sunday, we went to our old church. Gosh, it had grown so much in the time we'd been gone that they now had two services. The moment I walked in, my spirit was rejoicing. There were so many new faces. The familiar faces greeted us with hugs and smiles. It felt so good to be back in the House of God. I searched and searched for a particular friend but did not see her. During the service, the pastor asked us to stand. He told the congregation why we were back in town. He also shared with them that we had gone from being told Jack had six months to live to now finding out that he had lymphoma, which might be more manageable, and everything had been turned around. During the service, I looked at Jack's face. He was moved to tears. After the service, we spent a lot of time with the pastor and his wife. They prayed over us prior to our departure. My spirit was renewed like never before. As we were walking to our car, I saw a familiar car pulling into the parking lot. It was my friend, who I had been looking for in church. She had been told that we were still there meeting with the pastor and she came straight over. We embraced like little girls who hadn't seen each other in years.

Later in the evening, we went shopping for Quinton, and then we had to buy another suitcase because we had bought so much stuff to take home. When we returned to the room, I called the airline to find out how many miles were needed for an upgrade and if it was possible to upgrade. The representative told me we would be able to upgrade and it would cost us 25,000 miles each. "Great; we would like to upgrade to business class," I told her, and then I told Jack the business class upgrade on an international flight was heaven. I was feeling great knowing we would be able to rest on the flight back home without any crying babies next to us.

We woke up early Monday morning and had breakfast at our favorite pancake restaurant before heading to the hospital to pick up the test results. When we returned to the room, we went over all the paperwork. We didn't understand a lot of the medical lingo and all the numbers. We went back to the computer to research a lot of the terminology. From our limited knowledge and research, it appeared that this form of cancer was treatable, but it was still cancer. We checked out of the hotel and headed to the airport for our return flight. I just wanted to board the plane and get back home as soon as possible.

We finally boarded and it was great to be in business class. The treatment is so much better than economy class. We had linen napkins, real silverware, and a variety of foods to eat. As soon as I finished dinner, I took a sleeping pill. I was so tired that I passed on the dessert. I pushed a few buttons to change my chair into a flat bed, and then I went to sleep. That was the best sleep ever.

"Ladies and gentlemen, welcome to Johannesburg, South Africa." This was music to my ears. I was glad to see my son and dog when we arrived home.

The next day we returned to the medical unit to turn in the paperwork. The doctor told us that he would refer us to an oncologist, as they wanted to start treatment immediately. Later in the evening, we received an email from the embassy doctor that was forwarded from the medical unit in Washington, DC. The medical unit stated that Jack was not supposed to return to South Africa, but that he should have stayed in the United States for treatment. Jack and I became upset. We told the embassy doctor that we wanted him treated in South Africa. He relayed this information back to the medical unit in DC. The head doctor wrote back with an ultimatum stating that if Jack did not return to the United States for treatment, our tour of duty would be curtailed. "Can they do this?" I asked Jack. "Can they really make us go back? South Africa has some of the best medical doctors in the world. We're not in a third-world country." My mind started racing with thoughts of not being able to complete our tour. *Where are we going to live? Our house has renters in it. What about Quinton graduating from high school here?* I didn't want him to change schools in his last year. I didn't understand why the head doctor was insisting on Jack going back for treatment while Quinton and I remained in South Africa. I didn't know how they expected him to get back and forth to treatments, especially if he got sicker. Furthermore, where was he supposed to stay?

The embassy doctor made the appointment with the oncologist and told us to keep the appointment. My life felt so out of control. I began to get angry that somebody was making decisions for us without consulting us. I accompanied Jack to the oncologist. He was an older doctor who seemed very knowledgeable. He had reviewed Jack's tests and said that based on the results, it looked like Jack was in stage three or four. My heart sank and I fought back the tears. It seemed as though everything he said thereafter was in slow motion. I felt like I was in a bad dream and couldn't wake up. The doctor told us that Jack needed to have a scan done and a bone marrow test to accurately tell us what stage he was in. He made those appointments for us. Two days later, we were back at the hospital for the scan and the bone marrow tests. In the meantime, the DC medical unit was still fighting with us. I was so angry, tired, and fed up.

Dear God, you know our struggles. I cannot fight this battle alone. I turn this entire situation over to you, Lord. Dear God, if it is your will, please intercede and work this out for us.

I called my supervisor to update him on what was going on. He told me not to worry and if need be, Quinton could stay with him and his wife to finish the school year. I couldn't ask for a better supervisor and the support of his family.

We returned to the doctor for the results of the scan and the bone marrow test. The doctor confirmed that Jack had stage-three lymphoma. He said it had not spread into any major organs or into his bones. He was very optimistic. He said that he would recommend six to eight sessions of chemotherapy treatments. He told us the side effects of the chemo, including hair loss, loss of appetite, nausea, and vomiting. He assured us that this type of cancer was very treatable and has a high response rate to chemo. We told him that we had to get clearance from the medical unit in order to be treated in South Africa. We asked him to forward the treatment plan to the doctor at the embassy.

When I arrived home, I called my supervisor's wife and told her I wanted her to pray and be in agreement with me that we be allowed to stay in South Africa for Jack's treatment. I said, "D, I feel like the enemy is trying to come against us. I want you to pray this specific prayer with us. I don't believe this is how we are supposed to leave South Africa. I am claiming this victory as I turn this over to God because this is not my battle. It is too big for me." I then called my childhood friend and asked her to pray the same prayer. I don't know why out of all the people that had been praying for us that I only reached out to those two individuals.

Dear God, I'm so tired. I'm so drained that I don't feel like I have the energy to fight anymore. Dear God, please hear my cry. I know you didn't bring us this far to leave us. In the name of Jesus, I pray that you take this battle and this burden off me, Lord. You know our hearts, and you know our desires, Lord. Give us strength,

Lord, in the name of Jesus. Dear God, you said ask and it shall be given! I pray
these things in Jesus name, Amen.

I returned to work the next day. I tried to keep myself busy so I
wouldn't have time to think about everything that was going on. My
mind and body were exhausted. I found myself making careless mistakes. I started to cry. I closed my door to get myself together. I went
to my supervisor and told him I needed to go home. I just needed to
leave. "Terran, of course you can go home. Whatever time you need,
you got it, and we got you." I thanked him and gathered up my things.
I called Jack to let him know I was headed home. My head seemed to
be in such a thick fog. I couldn't remember how to get home. I managed to get myself back on track and made it home. I got into my bed
and cried myself into a deep sleep. Jack arrived home just as I was
waking up. He asked if I was okay because Quinton had called him
and told him he heard me crying. I assured him that I was okay and
I was just having a moment. He embraced me and assured me that
everything was going to work out.

Later in the evening, we got an email from the embassy doctor. He
forwarded an email from the doctor at the medical unit in DC. The
entire tone had changed. He stated that Jack could get his treatment
in South Africa if the South African doctor's treatment plan met US
oncology standards. The embassy doctor forwarded all the information back to the medical board for review. The next day, the doctor in
the United States personally called to say that Jack could get his treatment done in South Africa.

"Thank you Jesus, thank you Jesus, thank you Jesus!" I exclaimed
after hanging up the phone. Then I called my supervisor's wife to
share the news with her. "Faith of a mustard seed," she said. "Girl,
when this is all said and done, I want to be present when you all give
your testimony of how God has worked out this entire situation."

I was so overjoyed that I couldn't contain myself. I called my childhood friend who I had also asked to pray and be in agreement with
me. "My God, my God!" she stated. I told her I just knew that the
enemy had to leave us alone. "Ask not, want not," I said. After all the
excitement settled down, I told Jack that this battle was not ours and
God was showing us favor. He was also showing us He was in control

despite the things that were being told to us. I went on my social media page and posted the following update:

They said, "Stage 4 pancreatic cancer and six months to live."

God said, "I don't think so, test again…there is still work to be done."

They retested, retested, and retested, and scratched their heads in dismay.

God said, "My will shall be done."

Being mentally and physically drained we asked for an upgrade. They said, "Sure you can for 25,000 miles."

God said, "Rest—this one is on me. I will upgrade you AND you will retain your miles."

They were giving confusing and conflicting reports…

God said, "I am not about chaos and confusion."

They said, "Return to the US for more tests and treatment or else!"

God said, "Be still! The will of God will not lead you to a place where the Grace of God is not there to cover you."

They said, "Okay, you can remain in South Africa."

If you ask me why there is a pep in my step and a smile on my face, I will say I have an awesome and amazing Father who can do all things exceedingly and abundantly!

Everything started to work in our favor. We went back to the oncologist to schedule Jack's chemotherapy. He told us of all the side effects that Jack would experience. He assured us again that this was a very treatable form of cancer. He told us the chemo course would consist of six to eight treatments, and he didn't think Jack would be required to undergo radiation. We left the doctor's office with high hopes and high expectations.

The next battle we faced was dealing with the insurance company and the doctor's office that had never had an international patient. The first chemo date was getting closer and we still hadn't settled the details of the payment. When we arrived for the first day of chemo, there was still some confusion because the doctor's office had not received payment from the insurance company. Jack told them that if he had to pay for the first treatment himself, he would do it. They quickly consulted with the doctor, and he approved the treatment and said we could just pay our 15 percent co-pay as stated by our insurance.

The nurses escorted us to the treatment room, which was filled with big recliner chairs. We were the only ones in there at the time. I became sick at the stomach just being in that room, but I promised myself I wouldn't get emotional. This was so surreal. After months of testing, we were in this chemo treatment room. The nurses were very nice as they explained everything. They told us the chemo sessions would last about five or six hours. Jack told me I could return home instead of sitting there for such a long time. They got him relaxed in a chair and applied heat to his arm for the IV line. When they came back to start his drip, they explained that the first medication would make him sleepy as it prepared his body to receive the chemo. Then they returned with nine bags, and hung them on the IV pole. "My God, all that?" I exclaimed in surprise.

The nurse said, "Yes, all that and more."

After the nurse left the room, I took out my iPod and took a picture of all these bags, and then I took a picture of Jack. He told me to go home and rest until he was done. I bent down to kiss him and his body started jerking as if he was having a seizure. Then he started to laugh. I was so angry that I cussed him, and then I started to cry. I got up to walk out of the room and he called me back. He apologized for teasing me and asked me not to be so serious. He said he had to make some humor out of this.

I said, "It wasn't funny, Jack, and I'm already afraid because this is all so surreal to me now! Why would you do that knowing how I feel about things like this?" I looked at him and I could see the fear in his eyes too. His joke had been his way to mask his fears. I didn't want to leave him.

Nonetheless, he encouraged me to leave because he would be there for so many hours. It felt like one of the longest days of my life. It seemed like I was moving in slow motion the whole day. It was finally time to go get him. When I walked into the room, I saw that he was sleeping. There were bags of orange fluid hanging on the IV pole and another small clear bag. I walked over and gently kissed him on his forehead. He smiled as he slowly opened his eyes. "How are you feeling?" I asked.

"Tired and ready to go home," he said.

The nurse came over and said he had about a half hour more to go. I sat in the recliner next to him. He said he was hungry and asked if I could get him something to eat. I went to a fast food place just down the street. I came back and he was finishing up with the last bag. Just as he finished eating, the nurse came to remove the needle from his arm that was carrying the chemo into his body. As I sat there watching this unfold, I thought about how God has a way of showing us that we have the strength and power to deal with the things we fear the most and say we can't deal with. One of my biggest phobias and fears is dealing with sick people and taking care of them. I couldn't run away from this situation. God had placed it right in front of me to deal with. I could only pray that God would help me to be strong and make it through this process with my husband. In His own infinite wisdom, He knew He had already equipped me to do so.

Jack was finished and ready to go. He was a little weak, but he didn't show any other symptoms. As soon as we arrived home, he just wanted to lay down and rest for a while. He asked me to lay down with him. I laid there until he fell asleep, and then I eased out of the bed to prepare dinner. Later in the evening, I went to wake him for dinner. He said he felt so weak. We didn't expect this on the first treatment, as we had been told that the symptoms wouldn't start until the third or fourth treatment. I prepared his plate and brought it into the bedroom. I knew he must not have been feeling well because Jack has always been adamant about not eating in the bedroom or having food in the bedroom.

He stayed this way the entire weekend. I went to Quinton's room and had a long talk with him. I told him that his dad was weak, and as the treatments continued, he would become weaker, and I would need him to step up and help out around the house. I also told him that there would be times when his dad would look and feel fine, but he would have a lot of up-and-down moments. He said he understood, but I don't think it had really hit home just yet.

Just as Jack was getting his strength back, it was time for his second treatment. This time I didn't take the day off. I stayed until they hooked him up and he started to get sleepy. The nurse told me what time he would be finished. I returned to work and called to check on him. He was still pretty out of it. The nurse told me that the first medication, which prepares his body for the chemo, also makes him tired. When my workday was finished, I went to be with Jack and saw that he still had three bags to go. Once he finished, we returned home and he went to bed to rest a while. This time he slept longer than the first time.

I got on my computer and read an email from a mutual friend whose husband was diagnosed with lymphoma a few years ago. She was telling me her firsthand accounts of what to expect as we traveled on this journey. She told me how her husband was in and out the hospital on several occasions, and he experienced so much pain that he would just ball up in a knot. He wasn't able to work and he was constantly sick. She said it broke him down on every level, mentally, physically, and spiritually. She painted the worst picture of what it could be like for Jack. I wrote her back and thanked her for all the information. I also told her that it was our prayer that despite all the things we were told, God had us covered. I finished the email with this sentence: "It is our faith that is going to sustain us through this journey. The doctors have already been proven wrong on several occasions." I had to believe in my heart that God hadn't brought us thus far to leave us in the wilderness. I would not accept anything negative even though people's intentions were good.

After the second treatment, Jack started to experience discomfort and pain in his joints. He also went through a period of being constipated from the pain medications. One night he was in so much discomfort and all the stores were closed. I couldn't help him and I felt so helpless. The next morning I went to the pharmacy and bought some laxatives. They didn't work. I went to the store to buy some prune juice and apple juice. He had gone several days without moving his bowels, and it was becoming very painful.

I told him that if he didn't go in the next day I would have to take him to the hospital or the doctor. I also told him of an old southern remedy that would give him relief, but he was having no part of that. I guess in my desperation he thought he really needed to go before I pulled out some old tricks on him. He finally went and his stomach pains subsided. He was still having pain in his joints. The doctor had told us this would happen due to uric acid building up in his joints. He was given magnesium supplements to help, but they didn't seem to be working. I couldn't stand to see him in so much discomfort and pain.

One day I was on a social media site and read a blog about juicing. I started to do more research on the benefits of juicing. I ran out to the store and bought a juicer and lots of fruits and vegetables. I searched the Internet for different recipes and started to juice. We found that spinach was a natural laxative for Jack. I didn't think he was going to like it at first because it smelt like fresh-cut grass. He tasted it and actually liked it. If it was running low, he would ask me to make more. One of the nurses told me to add blueberries to the recipe. She also told me that juicing was a good idea because there would come a time when he wouldn't have the energy to chew food. I thought, *my God I'm going to be dealing with a child*. I quickly dismissed what I had heard. I couldn't let anything negative enter and linger in my thoughts. I started to see the benefits of the juicing. I even got Quinton into it. I wanted this to be a family thing. To my surprise, he actually liked it also. I then announced that I was going to change our diet. I was cutting out pork and beef from that day forward. I had to become creative in cooking with only chicken, fish, and lamb. I also added beans and pastas for protein. We were on a healthy roll and feeling great. The treatments continued one after another. The only side effect Jack experienced was extreme fatigue.

One day I received a text message that read, "We are praying for you and Jacky." It was from my friend's mother whose husband was fighting for his life with cancer. I was touched at how thoughtful this was of her to think of me when they were fighting the same disease. I responded and told her we were also praying for them. My heart was so full of joy. I found myself being more tired as I was doing more of the things Jack had usually done around the house. There were times when I felt like I couldn't breathe and I needed a break from everything and everybody.

One day I got a call from one of the trainers at the gym who was inquiring as to why I hadn't been to the gym in a while. I explained that a lot had transpired in the past few months, but I would return. Two weeks later, I decided to return to the gym and carve out that little time just for me. I had to keep myself mentally and physically healthy too. When I was leaving the building after completing my workout, I heard the trainer calling my name. As she approached me, she asked if she could pray for me. I was caught off guard because I didn't know her name, and I had only seen her a couple of times. I told her she could pray for me. She asked if it was okay to do so right there. Again, I told her yes. I raised my hand to hold her hand. She put her hand on my shoulder and began to pray. The tears started to flow. I felt such comfort and confirmation. I thanked her as we embraced. I later told my friends that God has a way of sending us gentle reminders that He knows our struggles, and He's got us in the palm of His hand.

Just as things seemed to settle down and we were becoming aware of the highs and lows of chemo treatments, I got a call from home regarding my mother. She had been informed that a fingernail infection that had not healed had spread and she would have to have her finger amputated. I immediately cried out to God in prayer. *Dear God, what is next? She's had toes and a leg amputated.* I kept in close contact with family members for updates. She had her finger amputated, but she was in a lot of pain. When I called her, she was screaming about how much pain she was in. I told her to return to the hospital and find out why was she still in so much pain. She didn't return initially. It took a lot of coaching to get her to go to the hospital. After talking to several family members, I learned that they seemed to think the doctor hadn't cut enough of the finger off. I felt like I needed to go home and take charge of this situation. I was torn between leaving Jack, who was not having a good week, and going home.

Jack could see my inner turmoil and urged me to go home. I started to plan my trip around Jack's next treatment. I went to work and informed my supervisor of my intention to return to the States to check on my mother's wellbeing. Once again, I had his support. He told me he thought I should go. His wife was assisting with getting

Quinton to and from work. She also offered to help in any way while I was gone.

This would be my third trip back to the States in two months. I don't like flying for emergencies. I arrived home, showered, and went straight to the hospital. It was good to feel the warmth of the sun in Florida. It was currently winter in South Africa, which means I had left a cold climate for a warm one, and the balmy temperatures soothed my soul. When I walked into the room, my mother was shocked that I had flown home. I had told family members not to let her know I was coming home. She was so glad to see me. Every time a nurse came into the room, she introduced me as her daughter from South Africa, not just her daughter. This told me she was very proud of me without ever saying it. I finally had the opportunity to speak with the doctor who performed the surgery. I explained that something was wrong for her to be experiencing the amount of pain she was having. After much debate, he told me he would have to operate again and remove the entire finger. He said he was planning to do the surgery on Thursday. I told him it would be great if he could do it then, as I was scheduled to fly out on Friday afternoon, and I wanted to be there for the surgery.

It was the Fourth of July, and I hadn't been home for a holiday in such a long time. I visited with my mother that morning and headed to my sister-in-law's house for a cookout. It was a hot summer day. I had forgotten how hot and humid it can be in Florida. We sat under the carport and were entertained by my nieces. I ate so much food and it felt good. Later in the evening, the kid inside me wanted to see the fireworks on the beach. It had been years since I had seen them and even more since I had been home to see them on the beach. I convinced my nieces to go to the beach with me. Everybody was reluctant to go because the traffic was terrible, and it would be difficult to find a place to park, but I wouldn't give up, and we set out for the beach. After driving around for a while, we found a parking spot but had to walk a distance to get closer to the beach. As we headed over the bridge, I looked back and saw a wave of people approaching like there was a mass exodus from the city. I could smell the hot salty air. I smiled as it brought back so many childhood memories of happy summers at my grandmother's house. It was magical.

The next morning I returned to the hospital before my mother was scheduled for surgery. She was in good spirits when they took her to the operating room. I told her I would be there when she returned. The surgery was successful. When she returned to her room, she wanted me to comb her hair and wash her face. She couldn't do some of the simplest things. My mother was so weak that she couldn't walk, not even with her prosthetic leg. I wanted to cheer her up, so I took her outside to get some fresh air, and I wheeled her around the hospital. When we returned to the room, the nurse came to change her bandage. My stomach turned in knots and I told her I had to leave the room. She knew I couldn't stay and watch.

After her dressing was changed, her lunch came and she refused to eat. She hadn't eaten any of her food. I felt like the mother talking to the child. "In order for you to regain your strength, you are going to have to eat something. Now I want you to eat something off this tray, and it is not going back with all this food on it."

"Okay, I think I can eat something," she said. Later in the day her bandage came off and I thought I was going to faint. I didn't look at her hand, and I wasn't about to wrap it. I frantically reached for the call button to call the nurse, and as I reached between the mattress and the wall, she touched my arm with her hand. Before I knew it, I said, "I'll slap the shit out of you! Why would you do something like that? You've been telling everybody how good I've been with you in the hospital, and you know I have a phobia of sick people, and you do this to me?"

"Hey, respect and honor your mother," she said.

"Don't provoke your children!" I responded. I wanted to run away from the hospital and not return. I called my sister and asked her when she was coming to the hospital. I felt like I couldn't deal with my mother at that point. I walked the halls of the hospital to get myself together. I returned to the room and just sat there. After some time had passed, I told her I was leaving because I was tired. I was back at the hospital early in the morning to visit her prior to my afternoon departure. I said my goodbyes to family members and headed back to the airport. I was so tired from the trip, but I was glad that I had come to be with my mom and everything had turned out fine.

Jack was waiting for me when I arrived. I took a deep breath and remembered why I loved South Africa so much. It was time to return to work and get back into the groove of things. Jack was doing well with his chemo treatments. He was feeling so good that he and Quinton went to play basketball. He came home with a busted lip as he said Quinton had charged him. I was so glad to see he had the energy to play basketball.

He completed his sixth chemo treatment on August 31, 2012 and was doing so well, but shortly thereafter, he began to feel weak. We celebrated his birthday on September 5 and had a good time at dinner. Later during week, he developed a slight fever. It wasn't high enough to warrant a trip to the hospital, but I kept a close eye on him and checked his temperature frequently. He stayed home from work and spent the weekend in the bed. He didn't have an appetite and he was becoming weaker. His fever was going up and down. Then it stayed consistently high. I called his oncologist and hold him how high Jack's fever had gotten. When the doctor asked if there were any other symptoms, I described how Jack had not been feeling well for the past several days. He told us to go to the hospital and have him admitted. He said he would call ahead so that the admission process would go quickly.

We went to the hospital and thought this was going to be a routine overnight stay to have some tests done and then be discharged. When we arrived at the hospital, they had received the order to have Jack admitted, but the receptionist stated she could not have him admitted unless they received a guarantee of payment since he was a private patient with no local health insurance. It was after working hours, and I knew that the embassy medical staff had gone for the night. I called my supervisor's wife, who happened to work in the medical unit, and I explained our situation. She stopped the doctor and another medical employee from leaving and told them about our situation. They immediately took care of the paperwork and faxed it over to the hospital.

With that issue resolved, an orderly came and wheeled Jack down to the oncology ward. They got him settled in his room with three other patients. This wasn't even a semi-private room. Four people to a room seemed a bit much to me, but this was not the United States. At

7:00 p.m., a guard came around and told me that visiting hours were over and I had to leave. I asked him to give me a few minutes, as Jack had just arrived to the room and I wanted to make sure he was settled. Jack told me he was okay and I should return home. I went home and packed a bag with his toiletries and pajamas to take to the hospital the next day. I returned to work and told my supervisor that they had admitted Jack and it should only be a day or two to run some tests on him to find the cause of his fever.

An overnight stay turned into several days. His fever stayed dangerously high and didn't go down. I called the embassy doctors and informed them that Jack had been in the hospital for a week and a half and there wasn't a break in his fever. They came to the hospital and asked to review his medical records. When I saw them, I felt like the cavalry had arrived. After reviewing his medical records, they informed me that the doctors were following normal protocol in treating his fever. They were giving him broad-spectrum antibiotics. They told me he should start to respond to the medication soon.

I was at the hospital every day to keep watch over Jack. His appetite slowly started to decrease. I arrived at the hospital on Saturday evening and noticed a big change in Jack. When he tried to drink a glass of water, his hands shook as if he had Parkinson's disease. He wasn't responsive to me, and he wasn't very coherent. I tried to make conversation with him, but his speech was delayed as if there was something wrong with him. I thought the fever had made him delirious.

I went back on Sunday only to find that his condition had worsened. I told the nurses of my concerns. They weren't aware of the changes I was seeing. I called Jack's oncologist only to find out that he was out of the country attending a conference. I was referred to another doctor in the practice, and I told him of my concerns. He told me he would see Jack in the morning. I called my friend from the medical unit and told her of the drastic changes I had observed. I asked her to come to the hospital, as I needed someone who was familiar with Jack to see him. When she arrived at the hospital, she immediately noticed a difference in him. I gave Jack a glass of water so she could see how his hands were shaking. "There is definitely something wrong," she stated. Jack wasn't his normal joking self. I tried to get him to talk, but he just laid there. I told him I had a sandwich that Quinton had made for him, but he never ate it.

Once again, I called the embassy doctors and asked them to examine Jack. They came to the hospital and noticed the difference in his condition right away. The oncologist informed me that he was going to have a neurologist examine Jack. He stated that Jack's cognitive function had been compromised, and he was fearful that the cancer had spread to his brain. Jack continued to talk in circles. I tried to engage him in conversation, but nothing was making any sense. I began to cry and there was no reaction from him. He just looked at me as if he didn't care. This wasn't my husband. My husband would try to console me or ask me what was wrong and why I was crying. There were no emotions coming from him.

The following day I met the neurologist, who performed a series of neurological tests on Jack. He then informed us that he wanted to do a lumbar puncture to test Jack's spinal fluid. He excused himself as he went to get the equipment. Jack told me he had to use the bathroom, and I helped him to the bathroom. He then wanted to brush his teeth. "The doctor has returned to do the spinal tap, sweetheart," I told him.

"He's gonna have to wait until I brush my teeth," Jack replied. "The doctors told me I need to brush my teeth every day," he said in a childlike voice. He wasn't leaving the bathroom until he brushed his teeth. The doctor was very patient as he waited. I helped get Jack back to the bed. Jack motioned for me to come close to him so he could whisper in my ear. "Are you going to leave me?" he asked.

"No, of course not; I'm going to be right here holding your hand."

"I don't know if he is really a doctor. He looks too young to be a doctor."

I smiled and told him he was a real doctor, and everything would be okay. We got him positioned in the bed and they administered medication to make him sleep. "If this hurts, then they are doing something wrong—you know that, right?" Jack said, and after he made that statement, he fell asleep. I sat in a chair next to the bed and held his hand.

The doctor began the procedure. He held the first tube of fluid up to the light. It had a yellow hue to it. I am not in the medical field, but I immediately knew that wasn't good. The doctor took several more tubes of fluid. Once the procedure was complete, he confirmed my suspicion. "Mrs. Jackson, your husband's fluid pressure was good. However, I'm concerned about the color of the fluid. I will send this to the lab, and we should have the results in the morning. He will more than likely sleep the rest of the night."

After the doctor departed, I sat there holding Jack's hand and said a prayer for him. I rubbed his head and told him he was going to be okay, and then I told him I love him. I left the hospital and phoned my supervisor to give him an update.

The next morning, when I entered Jack's hospital room, I saw that he was sleeping. The nurses told me that his fever had risen to 104 degrees. Despite the various types of antibiotics he was receiving, his fever was not going down. I was so fearful that the fever was going to affect his brain even more. As I sat there holding Jack's hand, he woke up. "Good morning, sweetheart," I said.

"Hey babe, how you doing?" he asked.

"I'm the one who should be asking how you are doing. Do you remember the procedure last night?" He didn't remember that he'd had a lumbar puncture. After I went over the event, he remembered some but not all of the procedure.

The doctor came in and greeted us. The look on his face was not a good one. "The results of the fluid came back late last night, and it tested positive for meningitis. This type of meningitis comes from the chicken pox virus." He asked if Jack had ever had chicken pox as a child, and I told him yes. He went on to explain that the virus never goes away. In a healthy person's body, it normally has no affect and just remains dormant. However, since Jack's immune system had been compromised by the chemotherapy treatments, the virus had surfaced. The doctor immediately started him on a different antibiotic. He explained that a specific antibiotic needed to be administered to treat meningitis.

Within two days, I could see a big difference in Jack's cognitive function. He was getting better! He could not recall the past two weeks. He didn't believe me when I told him he had been in the hospital for two weeks. A mutual friend came to visit and confirmed everything I had told him about the past two weeks. Jack remembered being admitted and thought he had only been in the hospital for two or three days. I continued to go to the hospital two or three times a day. Jack didn't want the hospital food so I brought him dinner every night.

All seemed to be going fine, and then he started to become weak again. He asked me to bring his walking cane from home because it was difficult and painful for him to walk. He became so weak that I started giving him a bath each night.

I initially though he was weak from being in the bed for so long. One night it took longer than usual to get him out of the bathtub. I sat him on the side of the tub while I dried him off. As we made our way slowly back to the bed, he said his leg was giving out on him. "Lean on me and we can make it to the bed," I said. He told me he didn't think he was going to make it. I gently let him slide down to the floor. "Nurse, nurse, somebody help me!" I yelled. Several nurses came in and asked what happened. Collectively we managed to lift him up and got him in the bed.

Once he was settled, I asked him what happened. "I just lost the strength in my leg and couldn't support myself," he said. I told him that he needed to walk and exercise his legs because he had been laid up for too long. I made sure he was okay before I left late that evening. He had been a patient for so long that the security guards did not run me out at the end of visiting hours the way they used to do.

I called Jack early the next morning, and he said he was fine. I went over for lunch, but he didn't feel like eating. He complained of being tired. He was so tired and weak that he couldn't make it to the bathroom anymore. The nurses gave him a urinal to use. Over the next several days, I noticed more changes. He wasn't eating the food I would bring from home. When he had to urinate, the sensation was at the last minute and he wasn't able to grab the urinal in time.

While visiting him, I encouraged him to sit on the side of the bed. When he tried, he told me his right leg felt very heavy. He couldn't move it. I swung his legs off the bed so they could touch the floor. He still could not move his leg. I called the nursed into the room to show them what was going on. They called the neurologist to inform him. The next day the neurologist examined Jack and noticed the loss of movement in his leg. The left leg didn't seem to be affected. He did not have an answer as to why Jack was losing movement in his right leg. He ordered another lumbar puncture to test the spinal fluid. There was still a yellow hue in the fluid. He ordered more medications and stated they would observe him closely.

Over next several days, Jack's condition continued to decline. Each day I went to the hospital became more difficult to see my husband fading away. A week later, he lost movement in his left leg.

Dear God, in the mighty name of Jesus, please heal my husband's body. I pray the doctors discover what is going on with him.

Jack had MRIs done one to two times a week. They revealed that his spine was inflamed and still nobody could tell us why. Soon Jack began to have bowel accidents so often that he had to wear adult diapers. He became increasingly weaker each day. He was always tired and slept most of the time, day in and day out.

One day he said to me, "Babe, I can't do this anymore. I'm so tired of fighting. Please let me go, and go on with your life. I'm so tired."

"If I give up on you, you will surely die. I can't give up on you! You are going to fight, and I'm going to fight with you! Don't you dare give up on me, because I haven't given up on you. I told you God is not going to take you away from me while Quinton is still a minor."

"I love you, sweetheart; please let me go. I feel like I'm dying, and I want you to prepare yourself. I want you to bring Quinton to the hospital to see me. I need to talk to him. Please call the rest of the kids for me. I need to talk to them before I die."

"Jack, I will bring Quinton here and I will call the kids because I will fulfill your wishes, but you are not going to die. God is not done with you yet!"

"Babe, please let me go. I want you to know that if I should die, I want to be buried at home. I've changed my mind about being buried here. It wouldn't be fair for the kids."

One by one, I called his kids in the States and left the room so that he could talk to them privately. The next day, I told Quinton that I was taking him to the hospital to see his dad because he wanted to have a talk with him. When we entered the room, I noticed immediately that Jack didn't look well. I whispered in his ear and asked him if he was okay and if he still wanted to talk to Quinton. He nodded yes. He told

Quinton to come closer. This was the first time Quinton had seen his father so ill. I had tried to shield him from how his father's health had declined. I didn't want him to worry and lose focus on his schoolwork. Quinton slid the chair closer to the bed and I left the room.

When I returned it was quiet. Jack asked Quinton to go get him a soda from the vending machine downstairs. When Quinton left, Jack broke down and started to cry. "Babe, please don't be so hard on him. He is going to be okay. I told him not to get angry if you found a boyfriend after I die."

"Jack, I'm not going to be with anybody else. You are going to make it through this season."

"I know, babe, but I want you to be happy and live your life. I'm releasing you. I don't want to die, but I'm okay with this."

We managed to regain our composure before Quinton returned. I sat there rubbing Jack's head and whispering how much I love him in his ear. The tears started to flow down his face. He told us to go home as it was getting late.

The next day was such a beautiful day. Jack had not been out of the bed or outside the hospital in three weeks. I called the nurses and asked if they would help me get him in a wheelchair so that I could take him outside to get some fresh air. It seemed like the longer he stayed in bed, the sicker he became. It took four of us to move him from the bed to the wheelchair. I took him into the courtyard with its beautiful flowers and lots of sunshine. When I went to move him into a shaded area, he asked me to leave him in the sun. It was beautiful to watch him soaking up the sun. I pushed him around the hospital and then back to the room. It seemed more difficult to get him back in bed than getting him out. He told us not to move him until his favorite nurse came to instruct us on how to do it properly. He enjoyed his outing, but it didn't last long. His health continued to decline.

The head embassy doctor came to visit us and told us that he wanted to med-evac Jack back to the States for better medical attention. We told him we wanted to think about it and discuss it. He stated there was no time. We asked him how soon he was talking about. "Sunday," he answered.

"Today is Friday," I replied. "I can't move that quickly as I have to make arrangements for my son and pack for the both of us." I felt like somebody had stabbed me in my heart. He wasn't taking no for an answer, and I don't like being pressured into decisions. I hadn't prayed and asked God for guidance.

Sunday morning arrived and I had not heard from the doctor. I phoned him and he said we would fly out on Monday. He told us we had a choice of flying commercial or on a medical air ambulance. The air ambulance flight would take over thirty hours because it was a smaller aircraft. The commercial flight would take twenty-four hours. He told us a nurse would escort us back to the States no matter which flight we chose.

Father God, please let me know if this is your will. I'm crying out to you, Lord, for a word, an answer. Dear God, I am being pushed and moved beyond my own understanding. Help me to understand.

As I sat in Jack's room, I held his hand and told him I wasn't sure about him going back to the States. He squeezed my hand and said, "You have faith right?"

"Yes," I answered.

"Okay, then let's do this," he said, and after that, I felt a little better.

I managed to get things in order. My supervisor picked me up and took me to the hospital. All the nurses came to say goodbye. We cried and hugged each other. I felt like I was leaving my family, as they had been so wonderful. Jack was all ready and we were just waiting for the nurse escort. I was told the individual's name was Jordan. I couldn't imagine how this nurse was going to help with rotating Jack on a stretcher for this long flight. The nurse arrived and it was a male. I was so glad and relieved. He introduced himself and explained the procedure. He met with the nursing staff and obtained all of Jack's records and medications. It was time to leave.

As they rolled him down the hall, all the nurses come out and lined the hall on both sides to say goodbye again and to give their well wishes. My supervisor's wife said she felt like she was with the First Family. After we exited the hospital ward, we went down to the oncology ward where Jack had received his chemo treatments. Again, the staff and nurses came out to give hugs and to say goodbye. Just as the ambulance staff got ready to put Jack in the ambulance, a nurse ran out yelling, "Wait…wait!" Jack's oncologist wanted to see him and say goodbye before we departed. He shook Jack's hand and told him to keep well. I hugged my supervisor and his wife. As we rode down the highway, all kinds of thoughts were running through my head. I felt like I was permanently leaving this country that I loved so much.

We arrived at the airport and the nurse escort got us settled in the infirmary. All our documents were checked and we were cleared to board the aircraft. A vehicle was parked at the rear of the aircraft. It lifted us to the rear door and the team got Jack on the stretcher for the long flight. Once we got him situated, I closed the curtains around him to allow him to rest and to keep other passengers from staring at him. We were ready for the first leg of this long flight. Germany was going to be our first stop and layover before hitting United States soil.

Dear God, please guide this plane safely to Germany. Please be with the pilots to allow them to guide this plane, Lord. Please cover this plane from the very tip of the nose to the very tip of the tail, Lord, in the name of Jesus.

The nurse kept a constant eye on Jack to ensure he was as comfortable as he could be. We turned him periodically to keep him from getting sore in one position. When it was mealtime, I fed him. Jack was thirsty, and there was no way of sitting him up. The airline didn't have any straws. Our angel escort was very creative. He took a breathing tube and cut it into a makeshift straw so that Jack could sip from a cup. As tired as I was, it was hard for me to sleep. I kept a close eye on Jack to make sure he was warm and comfortable.

We landed in Germany safe and sound. We disembarked the plane the same way we embarked. The medical crew and ambulance were waiting for us. It was freezing cold in Germany. They escorted us to the infirmary where we had a two-hour layover. After they came to get our passports, we got Jack settled in the bed and prepared to change his diaper. I put on gloves to help, but the medical escort told me he could do it by himself. I told him no, he is my husband and I want to help. I removed the adhesive and rolled Jack on his side to clean him up. I didn't expect his bottom to be so raw and red. My eyes filled with tears and sweat began to run down my face. I felt like I was going to pass out. The nurse told me he could do this and I didn't have to do this. Again, I told him no. We changed gloves three times in the process of cleaning him up. I felt so sorry for Jack because it was so painful. I reassured him constantly, telling him, "I'm so sorry, sweetheart, I'm almost done."

After we were done, I told the nurse I needed some air and a Coke. I felt like I couldn't breathe, but I knew I had to be strong for Jack. The escort got me a Coke, and I walked outside to breathe. The cold air felt so good. My legs felt like they were going to give out on me. I cried and asked God to give me strength through this process.

I returned to the room and kissed Jack on his forehead. The nurse escort filled out some paperwork, took Jack's vital signs, and administered his medication. We started to converse with each other. He told us he was getting married on Saturday. I asked if he would be saying the traditional vows. When he said yes, I told him that when he gets to the part about "in sickness and in health," to remember us and what we were going through. He also told us he was from Fort Lauderdale, Florida, and I told him I was from Delray Beach. He said he used to live in Delray at one time. As we talked about our journeys, we discovered he also lived in Pusan, Korea during the same time we were there. He was a young student at the time. I initially thought *what a small world*. Then I smiled and thought *God didn't send us a medical escort; He sent us an angel.* How ironic that we had so much in common with this total stranger.

Dear God, thank you for reminding us yet again that we are not alone, and you haven't forgotten about us.

It was time for us to depart again. We gathered all our things and proceeded to the ambulance that would transport us to the plane. This time passengers had started to board and were already on the plane. The flight attendants were wonderful. They ensured we were comfortable and assured we had anything we needed. I made sure Jack was comfortable and warm. I kissed him on the head and told him to hold on for this last part of the trip. It was another smooth flight. I was able to sleep during this leg of the trip. We finally touched down on US soil. Once again we exited at the back of the plane and were received by an ambulance as well as customs and immigration personnel.

I called my friend back in South Africa to obtain a number for patient relations at the hospital, as I didn't know where I was going to stay and hadn't made any hotel arrangements. I kept saying, "Okay God, work this out." We arrived at the hospital and got checked in. The nurse was running late to catch his connecting flight back to Florida because we were delayed in leaving Germany. He told us that he wasn't leaving until Jack was situated. He had started to check on alternate flights. I couldn't believe how dedicated and attentive he was. We exchanged business cards before he departed, and I told him we would meet again under better circumstances.

A nurse came and welcomed us to the hospital. She also informed me that I could stay in the room with Jack during his stay. Jack was so tired from the long flight. I just wanted to take a shower and rest for a while, but the nursing staff immediately started running tests and IVs. The patient representative came in and introduced himself, and told us if we needed anything, he was there to assist us. When he asked us if there was anything we needed or wanted, Jack spoke up. "Yes, I would really like a pizza. I haven't had an American pizza in years."

"Okay, Mr. Jackson, just tell me what you want on it and I will place the order for you."

"Jack I don't think he was talking about placing a pizza order and having it delivered to the hospital," I said, but I was wrong. Sure enough, he placed the order and they delivered the pizza to the hospital. I just shook my head in amazement. Jack was happy, but he only ate one slice because he was so tired.

After things seemed to slow down, I was able to shower and feel refreshed. While Jack was resting, I got on the computer to let family and friends know that we had arrived safely. Soon my cell phone started to ring nonstop from all the calls. I was so tired that I really didn't want to talk to anybody. I was just so overwhelmed with all the kindness and concern. Later in the evening, the nurses came and showed me how to let out the couch into a bed, and they gave me fresh linens and towels. I had a restless night, as the nurses seemed to come in the room throughout the night checking Jack's vital signs and running tests.

I was awakened early in the morning by a team of four neurologists. They performed several motor and neurological tests on Jack. They asked him about the events that led up to him being sent to Johns Hopkins Hospital. He couldn't remember anything except arriving at the hospital in South Africa. I had to fill in all the gaps for him. It was then that I was so thankful that I could stay in the room with him to be able to give the doctors his history. They also thought the cancer had moved to his spine. They ordered a series of blood tests along with a lumbar puncture. *Good lord,* I thought, *this will be his fifth spinal tap.* I know they had to run their own tests, but he had already been through so much. I provided them with all of Jack's X-rays, MRIs, bone marrow test results, and other medical documents. They said they would review all the material and consult with other doctors on the team. I kissed Jack on his head and told him everything was going to be okay.

"Come lay in the bed with me, please," he said. "I just want you next to me." It had been a month since we were in the same bed. I laid down next to him, and we just held each other until a nurse came in again to take his vital signs.

My phone rang and a lady introduced herself as Nic; she said she was with the Service. She said my previous supervisor contacted the Baltimore office and told them I was in their district at Johns Hopkins hospital. She wanted to make contact with me to see if I needed anything and to let me know that they were there to assist in any manner. The tears started to flow down my face as I thought how much the Service really does take care of their own. I told her I had made a rental car reservation at the Baltimore airport, and I would need a ride to pick up the car. She told me she would have an agent drive me to the airport. She told me his name and said he would contact me. I thanked her, and within moments, the male agent called me and told me he was downstairs in the lobby. "Wow, that was fast," I said, and then I told him I would be right down. I told Jack I was going to pick up the car and I would be right back.

As I was riding the elevator down, I realized I had forgotten to ask the agent what he was wearing. How would I recognize him? As soon as I stepped off the elevator and entered the lobby, I spotted him. He just looked like an agent. I approached him and asked if he was the agent I had spoken to, and he said yes. We walked outside to his car, and he said, "We are here to assist you with whatever you need." He drove by the office to show me where it was located. When we arrived at the car rental facility, I told him I had a GPS that would get me back to the hospital. He gave me his business card and the numbers to the office. I hugged him and thanked him for taking the time to get me there, and I assured him I was okay to get back.

On my way back, the GPS was giving me the wrong directions. I didn't know the address of the hospital and things got confusing. It was obvious that my maps were outdated. As I was trying to get my bearings, the phone ranged. It was Nic calling to see if I had made it back to the hospital. "Thank God you called!" I said. "My GPS is a little off, and I'm a bit lost." I told her what street I was on, and she guided me back to the hospital, staying on the phone with me the entire way. Soon the GPS was saying the same thing she was saying. "I think I'm on track now, Nic. Thank you so much!" She told me she would come to the hospital tomorrow to check on me.

I made it back to the hospital safe and sound. I told Jack of my experience and how the Service had stepped up to help me out. "God continues to show me that I'm not in this alone and He has not forgotten or forsaken me. He is such an on-time God." My old supervisor called to see how things were going. "Lyn, thank you so much for making the call and having the Baltimore office come to assist me."

"Not a problem!" she said. "I couldn't get down there, so I called and told them that you were in their district and I needed somebody to reach out to you."

"I couldn't believe it, but they were here to offer whatever assistance I needed," I reassured her. I was still amazed at how total strangers had come to my aid. *Thank you, dear God, for favor and watching over me.*

Family members and friends started arriving at the hospital. I was never alone. Everybody kept asking what I needed. The only thing I wanted or needed was for my husband to be okay.

Jack was unaware of the number of people that were coming to see him. He opened his eyes from time to time but wasn't very responsive. Then my old supervisor came to see us. "Sweetie, look who came to see you," I said to Jack. "Hey Lyn, you look good," he said. We smiled as I told her that she was one of the first persons he had recognized and acknowledged. Shortly thereafter, he went back to sleep, while Lyn and I sat there fellowshipping with each other. Jack's brother, sister-in-law, and cousins also arrived. The room was jam-packed. Jack was still unaware of all the visitors. We sat there talking and laughing. My spirits were lifted by all the love in the room. Lyn entertained us with stories of our South African experiences. It was so good to see her and laugh as we had so often done in our office.

One by one, everybody came and went. I took short naps in between the nurses making their rounds. All was quiet and calm, and then around eight in the evening, Jack started talking. I woke up to see what he needed and realized he was rambling again. Nothing was making sense. I lay back down and I heard him say, "Hi, Billy, yeah, come on in. Hey, Gregory, how you doing, man." My heart started to race, as these were his deceased nephews. *Dear God, please don't take him away from me, not now!* He was quiet for a while, and then he started rambling on and on again. Nothing was making sense. "I can move that box but it was too heavy. How many times can I tell you? When is it going to stop raining? Who is going to drive the car?"

"Jack, are you okay sweetheart?"

"Yeah, I just need to move some boxes." I sat there and listened to him go on and on. I then called for the nurses to come. I told them he was hallucinating again. I explained that he'd had an episode like this in South Africa. The nurse phoned the on-call doctor who came to examine him. Jack never stopped talking. The doctor ordered an emergency MRI. When they took him down, I managed to sleep for a few minutes. The neurology team arrived at around ten the next morning. I told them it appeared he was having some form of setback. They performed a variety of neurological tests and said he wasn't very responsive.

"Can you give him some type of sedative?" I asked them. "He hasn't slept for the past twenty-six hours, and I'm afraid he's going to crash and burn."

"I'm afraid we can't do that, Mrs. Jackson, because a sedative will interfere with the tests we have ordered for him today. He will eventually fall asleep on his own."

I wanted to ask if he could prescribe me something. The doctor told me he had ordered a full-body MRI for Jack, which would take about two or three hours. The positive side of Jack's cognitive dysfunction was that he wasn't aware that he is usually claustrophobic; thus, he didn't require a sedative for the MRI despite how long it would take.

When they took him out, I was able to get some sleep. One of Jack's cousins arrived shortly before they returned him to the room. He was alert but still somewhat delirious. He kept telling us he wanted to get out of the bed. I told him he couldn't get out of the bed. He replied, "Sweetheart, if you love me, you will help me get out of this bed."

"I do love you, babe, but you can't get out the bed."

A nurse walked in at that point and said, "Hello, Mr. Jackson, I've got your medication."

"I'm not taking no medication."

"Jack, you have to take your medication. It will help you get better."

"Nope, I'm not taking it," he said in a childlike voice.

His cousin tried to convince him to take the medication, but he refused. Then he decided to strike a bargain. "I'll take it if you let the bed rails down and let my feet hang out." The nurse agreed and lowered the rail. Jack turned to me and whispered in my ear, "Now help me get out."

"Mr. Jackson, I can hear you," the nurse said. We all started laughing.

"Shit," he said.

"Jack, I'll take my medicine if you'll take yours. Look, I'm taking mine now. I need for you to take yours."

"That's good, sweetheart, but I'm not taking it." The nurse had told us that if he didn't take his medicine, they were going to put a tube down his nose to administer the medication directly to his stomach. After an hour, he gave in. The nurse put the pill in his hand, and he started talking to his cousin and making us laugh while trying to put the pill in the pocket of his gown.

"Okay, I took it; can I get out now?"

"Mr. Jackson, you didn't take it, you were trying to put it in your pocket, and it fell out." He laid back and started to push himself out of the bed.

"Jack, if you don't take this medicine, they are going to put a tube down your nose, and I know you won't like that. Please take the medication." He finally took the medication. The nurse thanked him and left. His cousin and I laughed about the incident. A few hours later, the nurse returned and told us they were moving him to a room closer to the nurse's station so they could keep a closer eye on him to make sure he didn't try to get out of the bed. We quickly packed up his belongings. As they were rolling him down the hall, he yelled out my name.

"I'm right here, Jack," I called out.

"Oh, I feel cool. Is my dick hanging out?"

"Jack! No it is not, sweetheart!" We all began to laugh and shake our heads.

We got him settled in the new room, and he promised not to try to escape from the bed. It was funny how his voice had changed. So many things about him were changing. In the midst of his health crisis, he still managed to make me laugh. Inside he was still Jack. We had visitors coming every day. I was drained and I knew he had to be also. So many people wanted to come and offer their support and to see him since were back in the United States.

Jack had longed to see all his children while he was in the States. His oldest son and his wife came often, but he hadn't seen the middle and youngest children. His second son came from Texas. He brought his mother, grandmother, sister, and his sister's three kids. I told Jack that his ex-wife and mother-in-law were coming to see him.

"Babe, please be honest with me. Am I dying and you're not telling me?"

"No; why would you ask something like that?"

"Didn't you say my ex is coming from Virginia and her elderly mother is coming to see me?"

"Yes, Jack, they just want to see you. We're all family; why wouldn't she want to come see you? Trust me, you are fine."

When his son arrived, he tried so hard to hold back the tears. He didn't expect to see his father in this condition. He left the room and

I followed behind him. We went to the lounge area and sat there for a while until he was able to get himself together. I told him that his father was actually doing much better than before, and I assured him that everything was going to be alright. My heart went out to him because he is the emotional one of all the children.

Jack got to see his daughter's three children, and he also got a chance to see the latest grandbaby that was named after him. He was in heaven, and it really gave him so much joy.

Day in and day out, visitors came and prayed with us and for us. We had so many visitors that people had to take turns to come inside the room. One Sunday, an old colleague from South Africa came while we had a room full of family and friends. We all gathered around Jack's bed and held hands as our friend prayed. The atmosphere was so full. You could feel the spirit moving in the room. It was such an awesome and uplifting moment. I felt like we had church right there in the room. It was good to see so many of Jack's family members that I had not seen in years. It was good to see one of my dearest girlfriends and her family. Whatever I needed, she would send it to me. I was so grateful and overwhelmed with all the support.

Time was winding down. I woke up and Jack wished me a happy birthday. He remembered my birthday. There were so many things that he couldn't remember, but he remembered my birthday. I gave him a big hug and a kiss and thanked him for remembering. I told him I was going to treat him to a special breakfast. I went out and found our favorite pancake restaurant, and placed an order to go so that I could bring it back to the room and share it with Jack. He didn't eat much, but it was good to see him eating more than usual. He fell off to sleep, and I took a nap too. I was taking short naps whenever I could get them in. Between visitors and nurses coming in and out of the room, I wasn't sleeping much at all.

I was awakened by a knock at the door. When the door opened, several nurses, techs, and staff members started singing "Happy Birthday." They had a cake and a card signed by all the staff. I started to cry. "How did you all know?"

"Mr. Jackson told us it was your birthday, and we wanted you to have a special day today."

"This is too much; thank you so much." We took pictures and had a wonderful time. I was so in shock.

"I couldn't go out and buy you anything," Jack said, "but I wanted you to have a beautiful day."

"Oh, sweetheart, this is the best birthday I've had." I gave him a big hug and kiss. I couldn't believe he was thinking of me even being in the state he was in.

Later in the day, I was leaving the room when a nurse stopped me as I approached the sink to wash my hands. "Where you going?"

"Excuse me?" I replied, not believing she was speaking to me with this tone.

"Where are you going?"

"I'm over forty years and then some, and today is my birthday. I don't think I need to tell you where I'm going."

"Okay, Mrs. Jackson," she said.

I proceeded downstairs, and when I returned to the room, there were flowers all over the place, another cake, a bottle of wine, and more birthday cards. Jack's cousins were in the room, and as soon as I entered, they started singing "Happy Birthday." I started crying again. "How did you all do all this when I was only out of the room for a minute?"

"We were in the family lounge" one cousin stated. The room door opened, and I saw the nurse I had just given a hard time about where I was going. She smiled and explained, "I thought you were going into the family lounge, and I was trying to stop you because they were in there with all this stuff."

"Oh sweetie, I'm sorry," I said. We all just started laughing. This was so unexpected. Now I had two cakes. Later in the day, Jack's oldest son, daughter-in-law, and her mother came with the kids. They brought me two cakes.

"Good Lord, what am I going to do with all these cakes?"

I really felt loved this day. I brought a cake into the family lounge and told the staff to please eat it. We gave cake to all the visitors that came that day. At the end of the day, I still had two cakes left. It was a wonderful day.

When everybody finally left for the night, I was ready to get some sleep. The last visitor left around 11:00 p.m. This hospital did not have visiting hours and people really took advantage of this. Jack's cousin was still with us. Around 11:30 p.m., the room door opened. "Hi, I'm the sitter."

"The what?" I asked.

The lady backed out of the door way and looked at the nameplate on the wall. "Is this Mr. Jackson's room?"

"Yes it is, and I'm Mrs. Jackson; may I help you?"

"Yes, I'm hired to sit with you."

"Sit with me for what?"

"Let me go talk with the nurse."

Jack's cousin and I just looked at each other. We were completely baffled. The nurse returned with the sitter and explained that they thought I could use a break, so they hired a sitter to come into the room and sit with Jack to allow me to get some rest.

"Excuse me, but I didn't request a sitter."

"Yes, we know, but she can sit here and attend to Mr. Jackson during the night, and you can rest."

"First, I don't care if Jesus was here to sit. If my husband needs attention, I'm still going to get up. Secondly, I didn't ask for this lady, nor do I want her services. I'm not sleeping in here with a stranger watching me."

"So you don't want the service?"

"No I do not."

"Okay, sorry to disturb you, Mrs. Jackson."

Again, Jack's cousin and I just looked at each other. It would have been different if they had offered this during the day to allow me to leave the hospital to run errands or to get a short break. Jack's cousin left and I was finally able to sleep.

The next morning the neurology team arrived. They did their usual cognitive testing and asked a lot of questions. When the doctor asked Jack to move his feet, he had movement in his left foot. "I can move it!" Jack exclaimed.

"Try moving your right foot." There was no movement in his right foot.

"Well there is some improvement," the doctor said nonetheless.

I asked, "Can you explain why he lost movement in his legs, and now he has some movement in one foot?"

"No, unfortunately we still don't know why he lost movement, let alone why or how he regained partial movement in one foot. We're going to run more tests, and we are adding some infectious disease specialists to the team to see if there is anything they can come up with."

We thanked them and they departed. I looked at Jack and said, "I don't understand how we're in one of the best hospitals in the world, and they too cannot find the cause of the loss of movement in your legs. In the end, I believe they will never know and you will walk again, and only God can and will get all the glory."

Once again, a series of tests was run and nothing came back abnormal. Jack had been stuck so many times that he had run out of veins. His poor arms were so bruised. I just wanted to pick him up out of that hospital bed and bring him back to South Africa. The infectious disease team ran tests for rare diseases that can be contracted outside of the United States, and everything else under the sun. Still nothing came back abnormal.

My time was winding down and I became sad at the thought of leaving my husband behind. I had taken care of him night and day. I had become his voice and his advocate. I did not yet have a return ticket to South Africa. When I started calling around for my return orders, I kept getting the runaround. Each person I spoke to told me another person was responsible for my return flight. I was getting angry and upset regarding this entire process. We had been rushed out of South Africa, and now nobody seemed to know how to get me back. After several phone calls to the embassy in South Africa and to Washington, DC, I got a call stating my orders had been approved and

I would fly out the next day. I was departing days before our wedding anniversary. This would be the first time in twenty-three years that we would not be together on that special day. My heart was so heavy.

The next morning, I woke up early to get some last-minute things packed. When I looked at Jack, I could see the sadness on his face. "It's going to be okay," I reassured him. I don't know if I was trying to convince him or myself. We spoke very little that morning. It seem like the more I talked, the more I felt the tears starting to flow.

"Come get in the bed with me please," Jack said softly.

I laid there in his arms and closed my eyes. The tears started to flow. "I love you so much, sweetheart. I'm coming back for you."

"I know. I love you so much, babe, and I'm so thankful for all that you have done throughout this process. It is my promise to you that I'm going to get you that Mercedes SLK you've always wanted. You really deserve it. I don't think I could have made it through this process without you."

The staff came to say their goodbyes with lots of hugs. "You all better take care of him until I return," I reminded them.

"We will, Mrs. Jackson. He's in good hands. We'll have somebody take your bags downstairs for you. Take care, and safe travels."

"Well, sweetheart, this it. I'm going back to be with Quinton, but you know I'll be on the next thing smoking if you need me."

"I know, sweetheart, you be safe, and call when you arrive." We kissed and hugged each other for what seemed like a lifetime.

"I love you."

"I love you too."

I managed to get myself together, and I made it to the airport in time. I sat in the airport and listened to my music. Just before it was time to board, I prayed.

Dear God, please look after Jack. Give us the strength to make it through this valley. Lord, you know my heart is so heavy right now. Please give me peace. Dear God, my faith is all I have right now, and I'm putting all my trust in you. Please heal Jack's body and restore him. Touch him in that hospital bed and heal him in Jesus name.

As I walked down the tunnel to board the plane, I felt like I was leaving my best friend behind. I didn't know what was going to happen to us. I didn't know what the future had in store for us. I didn't know a lot of things. I didn't have answers for so many of my questions.

What I do know is that I will continue to walk in the steps that were ordered for my life. Even though I'm not certain where they will lead, I will continue to press on. I will continue to walk and gain Wisdom While Walking.

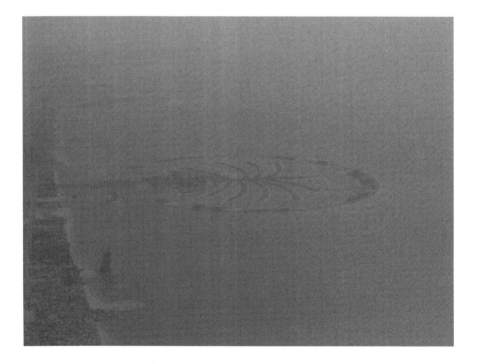

Made in the USA
Charleston, SC
16 October 2013